KAZAKHSTAN

FLINT RIVER

KAZAK

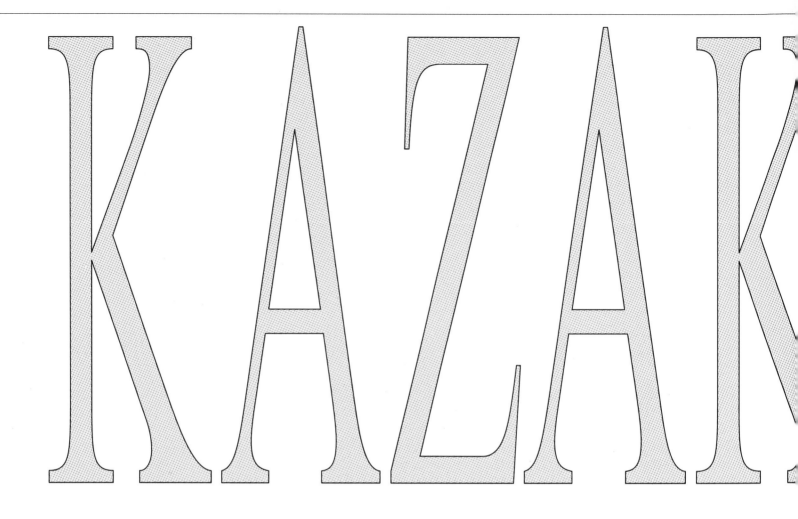

Text by

Klara Serikbaeva

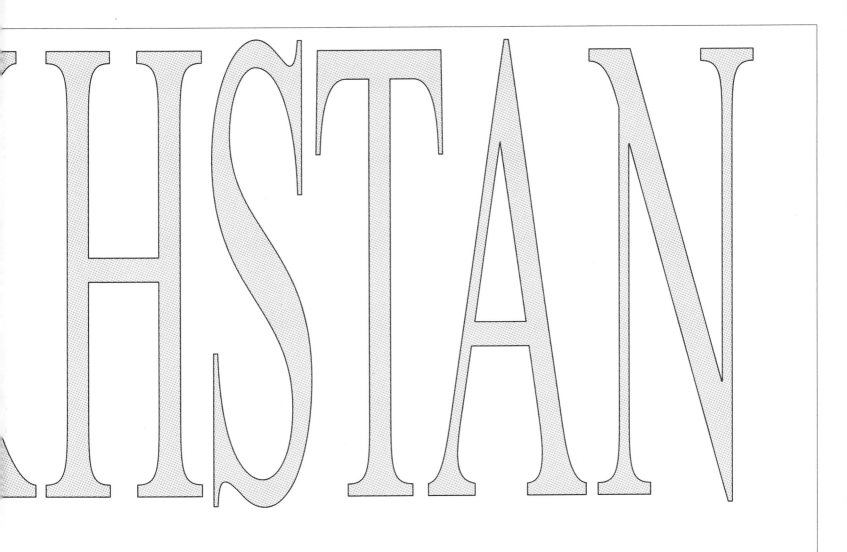

Photographs by

Dragoljub Zamurovic

A Motovun Group Book

© Flint River Press Ltd, 1995

Published in English, Russian and Kazakh by
Flint River Press   EL Bureau
28 Denmark Street   Gornaja 97
London WC2H 8NJ   Almaty

ISBN: 1-871489-24-5

Design
Gane Aleksic

Translated from the Russian by
Richard McKane

Editor
Madge Phillips

Additional photographs by
Victor Gritsyuk
Alexander Dzhus
Paul Harris

Black-and white sketches by the great Kazakh scholar Chokan
Valikahanov are used in this book

Typset by Avalon, London

Colour separation by Grafika
Ilirska Bistrica, Slovenia

Printed and bound in Slovenia by
Tiskarna Ljudska Pravica, Ljubljana

CONTENTS

FOREWORD

I accepted with pleasure the invitation to write a short Foreword to this book on Kazakhstan, which has been prepared for publication by Kazakh and British publishers. In my view this book will be useful, above all, because it will acquaint the foreign reader with our country, its prospects for development, and with the learning, culture and traditions of this multinational state. This would seem to me to be very timely. It is very important that the world should know more about Kazakhstan, the progress of its reforms, the country's potential, its efforts for peace, and the lives and problems of its peoples.

We need to stimulate interest in order to broaden co-operation on all levels between Kazakhstan and foreign partners and to attract further foreign investment. It is also important that we expand our political, cultural and information dialogue with other states.

Readers will probably be familiar with the processes taking place in the former state of the Soviet Union. Each republic has its own specific features, but there is also much in common. We are all moving towards a market economy, building our statehood under the difficult conditions created by the severance of the former strong ties. However, the countries of the Community are striving to overcome the processes of disintegration. Success in this will undoubtedly depend on the stabilization of the individual economies, the creation of normal conditions of life on a purely human level, and the free movement among states that were once completely open to each other.

It should be emphasized that in Kazakhstan there are favourable conditions for positive change in the social, economic and political spheres, which permit an optimistic view of the future. These favourable conditions are the geographical position of the republic, its huge natural riches, a highly-educated population, and the stable socio-political atmosphere.

The reforms which we are undertaking are aimed, in the first place, at creating a basis for a market economy, the democratization of public life, and the foundation of an appropriate legal system. We are endeavouring to make more effective use of our economic and production potential, while at the same time promoting the spiritual values of our society and unity among the many nationalities. We are learning to look more widely at the world, keenly observing the experience of other countries, and we are dedicated to creating truly democratic state institutions.

In pursuing the modernization of our young sovereign state—and by this I mean modernization in all areas: technical, economic, political—we are not blazing a new trail, but following a road that has already been laid down by mankind and the civilized countries. I am convinced that step by step we will reach world standards in all these respects.

I am an active supporter of the reforms, endeavouring to make Kazakhstan a country of international standing and ensure that it will not repeat the mistakes of the recent past, with its irrational experiments, its forgetfulness of the national traditions and cultural heritage.

In this respect, 1995 is a special year: the 150th anniversary of the birth of our great poet and thinker, Abai. For the first time Kazakhstan is commemorating Abai on an international level, for UNESCO has declared this to be the Year of Abai. We are grateful to this important international organization for extending its support to the celebrations.

I am convinced that this event will give a powerful impetus to the development of the artistic and moral potential of the people of Kazakhstan, and to the rebirth of national consciousness. The scope and profundity of Abai's thought is such that all who know his work will come back to it again and again throughout their life. If every one of us lives only a small part of our lives under the aegis of this great man, our nation will pass the test of spiritual strength.

I would also sincerely like to thank the British publishers, Flint River Press and Philip Wilson, as well as the Kazakh EL Bureau and Rollan Seisenbaev, who have helped to publish Abai's work. This is of mutual benefit: Kazakhstan gains an intellectual product of a high standard, and the western reader, I hope, will gain an insight into our cultural heritage. I would like to hope that our foreign visitors and readers will not be so preoccupied with practical matters as to neglect the many other aspects of life that will give them an understanding of the soul of our people.

Historically, Kazakhstan, located at the meeting place of two cultures, has absorbed many aspects and valuable features of both, and has become a truly multinational state. People of more than a hundred nationalities now live in the republic. The Kazakhs are the most numerous, followed by the multi-million Russian diaspora, Ukrainians, Germans, Azerbaijanis, Uygurs, Koreans... Over the ages they have all settled on the welcoming expanses of the Kazakh steppe. Many have come in more recent times—to open up the virgin lands and to develop industry.

It must be said that there are black pages in the history of my country. It is enough to recall the forced collectivization of the 1930s, when thousands upon thousands of my fellow-countrymen lost their lives and many Kazakhs were sent into exile.

It is well known that whole nations were exiled to Kazakhstan in the Stalinist years. However, they were not treated as aliens here—nobody has ever held a grudge against the Kazakh people. I can state with conviction that there has always been a genuinely friendly atmosphere in the republic.

We are also striving to establish ourselves as a peace-loving state in the international arena. When the question of the fate of nuclear weapons in the former Soviet republics was raised, Kazakhstan showed its good will by voluntarily signing the nuclear weapons non-proliferation treaty. In December 1994, at the summit meeting attended by the USA, Great Britain and Russia, a memorandum was accepted guaranteeing the security of Kazakhstan, Ukraine and Belarus. With this act, a significant phase was concluded in the realization of the combined efforts of our countries to achieve a more secure and stable world order. I regard every official visit I make to any country as an opportunity for furthering efforts in this direction.

It was Kazakhstan that put forward a proposal to convene a conference, similar to the European Conference on Security and Co-operation, to discuss measures to increase mutual trust and security in our huge region. Likewise, the idea of forming a Eurasian Union has as its aim the strengthening of international ties among the members of the CIS and those states wishing to join it, the elimination of sources of tension in the post-Soviet era, and the establishing of friendly relations between peoples.

I have only briefly talked about Kazakhstan today, but I hope that this book will significantly broaden the reader's knowledge of our country. It is my sincere wish that citizens of other countries will find here loyal friends and partners, and that bonds of friendship, mutual understanding and collaboration will bring us closer together.

I take this opportunity to wish you all peace, happiness and prosperity.

Nursultan Nazarbaev
President of the Republic of Kazakhstan

22nd March 1995

LAND AND PEOPLE

1. The territory of Kazakhstan has great variety of vegetation and relief: rolling grasslands, towering mountains, forested hills and sandy deserts. It covers an area of over 2.7 million square kilometres, the size of western Europe. In the picture: the canyon of the River Charyn.

Kazakhstan, a land of ancient civilization in the Central Eurasian region, has a remarkable history. In this vast expanse, through which passed major trade routes linking East and West, the nomadic and settled worlds came together over the centuries, powerful empires and states rose, perished and rose again from the ashes, cultures and religions developed and were enriched by mutual contacts.

The Kazakhs never started wars. They stubbornly and bravely warded off the invasions of their restless neighbours, and defended the borders of their homeland, valuing their freedom and independence more than life itself. Love of peace is imbedded in the national character and guides the formulation of state policy today, which is based on the principle of peaceful co-existence with all mankind.

The wide, hospitable steppe, the home of nomads who had lived for millennia in complete harmony with the laws of nature and never built prisons or houses of detention, was fated in the last half century to be turned by the authorities into a vast nuclear testing ground of international significance, possessing the terrible power to destroy life on the planet for all eternity. But this was not by the will of the Kazakh people.

Having survived the cataclysms of the twentieth century and started a new life on the threshold of the new millennium, Kazakhstan, with all its original, flourishing and rich culture, its age-old traditions and fascinating history, is opening up to the world. By its efforts, it hopes to help in building a world without slavery and violence, a world in which work and culture are united, to serve the cause of beauty and nobility of spirit, to join with all progressive humanity under the banner of universal harmony.

Independent Kazakhstan is a multinational state, in as far as its population is made up of a hundred nationalities, but it is also the state of the Kazakh nation. The ethno-cultural affirmation of the Kazakhs in no way restricts the national values and rights of other peoples who live or come to settle in the republic. The Constitution of the Republic of Kazakhstan guarantees the all-round development of all nationalities and citizens, and the creation of decent living conditions for everyone. The young state is now passing through the very difficult period of formation, and the path to the attainment of its goals may prove to be a long one, but the people of the republic are fully determined to press on to the end.

'We must start out on that path if we truly want to rise from our knees and live normally.' These words of the first President of the Republic of Kazakhstan, Nursultan Nazarbaev, express the will and desire of the whole of the population to build a better life for their children and future generations.

Relief and Climate

The Republic of Kazakhstan is located almost in the centre of the Eurasian landmass. Its territory stretches from the lower reaches of the River Volga in the west to the Altai Mountains in the east, a distance of 3,000 kilometres, and from the Western Siberian plain in the north to the peaks of the Tien Shan, 1,600 kilometres away in the south. The total length of its frontiers is over 15,000 kilometres, of which over 3,000 are on water.

In the west and north, Kazakhstan borders on the Russian Federation, in the south on Turkmenia, Uzbekistan and Kirgizstan, in

*2. The monument to the great Kazakh
poet, Abai, in Almaty, facing the mighty
peaks of the Alatau.*

3. Sections of a canyon rise above the surroundings like the towers of medieval fortifications. The popular name for this place is 'Kum Kala' meaning Sand Castle.

4. On the road to Taldy-Korgan, a south-eastern province of Kazakhstan not far from the border with China (overleaf).

5. The River Charyn, which flows through the eastern part of Almaty province, is a tributary of the Ili, one the country's biggest rivers, which feeds Lake Balkhash. (pp. 14-15)

6. *A herd of camels grazing beside the River Ili at sunset (previous pages). Camel breeding is an important sector of livestock rearing in Kazakhstan.*

7, 8. Twilight on the dusty Kazakh steppe, when the cries of the herders echo across the plains as they round up their livestock.

9, 10. Kazakhstan has four main climatic-vegetation zones: wooded steppe, grassy or open steppe, semi-desert and desert. The wooded steppe is found in regions with higher precipitation, mainly in the north.

*11, 12. The Moyunkum Desert in the
south of Kazakhstan comprises both
sandy massifs and rolling dunes.*

13, 14. Although Kazakhstan has almost 50,000 lakes, both freshwater and saline, and nearly 85,000 rivers, huge areas are arid and prone to drought. High summer temperatures drastically affect the water level of many lakes and rivers.

15. Between the Caspian and Aral seas stretches the great Ustyurt plateau, which in ancient times was the cross-roads of caravan routes.

16. A special type of fine-fleeced sheep which stores reserves of fat in its tail is raised in the arid regions of the republic where grazing is sparse.

17. Winter on the slopes of the Talgar Alatau Mountains in the far south of the country, where the highest peaks are to be found.

18. The huge Chimbulak glacier, at a height of 3,150 metres in the Zaili Alatau range. In the mountainous south and south-east of the country, there is an area of over 20,000 square kilometres of permafrost.

*19, 20. The road to Chimbulak, a
mountain famous for its gigantic
glacier (above), one of over two
thousand in Kazakhstan.*

21. Lake Jalanash in the beautiful wooded lake district of Kokshetau in the north of Kazakhstan, an area with enormous tourist potential.

22. Lake Almatinskoye, south of the capital, is a reservoir supplying water for the capital, but also a popular recreation spot which offers excellent fishing.

26. The shores of the Aral Sea have receded by 60 to 120 kilometres in recent years, as a consequence of excessive drawing of water from the rivers that feed it. The result is an ecological disaster.

27. Canals are of major importance for irrigation in drought-prone regions where agriculture would otherwise be difficult or impossible to sustain.

the east on China. The total area covered by the republic is over 2.7 million square kilometres: France, Portugal, Spain, Italy, Greece, Sweden and Finland taken together would fit into its territory.

Administratively and territorially, Kazakhstan is divided into 19 provinces and two cities. However, according to natural conditions, resources and economic specialization, it comprises five economic regions: Western, Northern, Central, Southern and Eastern.

The broad territory of Kazakhstan is notable for the variety of its relief, ranging from low-lying plains to towering mountains. Almost a third of its area is lowlands, while upland plains, plateaus and hilly massifs up to 600 metres cover half the country. One fifth of the territory is mountainous, though high mountains (over 2,000 metres) account for only one tenth of its area. There is a general rise in altitude from the western and northern regions of Kazakhstan to the eastern and south-eastern.

Low mountains (500 to 1,000 metres) are to be found in various regions. In central Kazakhstan the broad plains merge into low massifs and towards the south and south-east extend to the mountain systems of the Altai, Sary-Tarbagatay, Jungar Alatau and Tien Shan. A number of peaks in the Tien Shan, Jungar Alatau and Altai reach 4,000 metres. The highest point is Khan-Tengri (6,995 metres) in the Tien Shan, on the border with Kirgizstan.

A striking feature of Kazakhstan's relief map is the preponderance of plains: the Caspian Depression (Syrt), the area of Western Siberia in the north, the Ustyurt and Torgay plateaus, the Turanian lowlands north and east of the Aral Sea, and the Moyunkum Desert. The lowest area in the republic and the whole of Eurasia, 132 metres below sea level, is around the Caspian Sea.

The climate is predominantly extreme continental, and very prone to drought owing to the country's position in the centre of the Eurasian landmass: it is 2,000 kilometres distant from the Black Sea, 3,000 from the Baltic and Arabian seas, and 5,600 kilometres from the Sea of Japan.

Kazakhstan has all types of climate except arctic, tropical and equatorial. Broadly speaking, there are four main vegetational-climatic zones: wooded steppe, steppe, semi-desert and desert. The wooded steppe zone is in the far north of the republic, in the lowlands which have the most water. The steppe zone covers large areas in the north, while the semi-desert climate occurs in the dry steppes in the central part of Kazakhstan. The desert zone comprises much of the plains and consists of three types of desert: clay, sandy and stony.

Winter lasts for four to five months in the steppe zone, with temperatures falling as low as minus 45°C, and in the semi-desert and desert three or four months. In the mountainous regions precipitation is higher in this season, and towards the south the winters become milder.

Spring is fairly brief in all the zones, with a duration of one to two months.

Summer, which lasts about five months in most regions, brings more frequent rain and strong western winds to the wooded steppe and steppe zones. In the plains and regions of low mountains, precipitation is slight and the weather is generally hot and dry. The length of summer in the mountains depends on altitude: at greater heights the weather becomes progressively more cloudy and the temperature can fall to freezing point.

28. As a result of the shrinking of the Aral Sea, 25,000 square kilometres of dry seabed are exposed, from which 75 million tons of sand, dust and salt rise into the atmosphere each year.

Autumn comes to the north at the beginning of September, to the central area in the latter half of the month, and to the south at the end of October. In general the weather is overcast, with precipitation and cold winds.

The annual number of clear days ranges from 120 days in the north to 260 in the south; in the Balkhash depression there are, on average, only 10 overcast days in a year. The territory of Kazakhstan as a whole suffers from a severe drought problem: in the last two decades there have been four years of drought. The relief of the area is decisive in the distribution of precipitation. The lowest rainfall is round Lake Balkhash—100 to 125 millimetres a year, but close to the mountain peaks the annual precipitation rises sharply to 1,500 millimetres.

In the mountain regions, strong winds and blizzards are frequent in the colder seasons, and hail is not uncommon. Winter storms also occur in the desert and semi-desert zones. The steppe regions suffer from dust storms, which can last for up to a month and a half. Mists usually descend in the spring and autumn periods. The most unpleasant phenomenon for livestock raising is icy ground: a layer of ice, up to 22 centimetres thick, is formed when the temperature drops after mist or rain.

Rivers

The water resources of Kazakhstan are very unequally distributed. The glaciers located in the south and east of the republic are the main source of water for the rivers that flow north and west. Most of the country's 2,724 glaciers are in the Jungar Alatau, Zaili Alatau (i.e. Alatau beyond the River Ili), Kungya and Terskya Alatau mountains. The biggest is the valley glacier in the Talgar massif, which reaches a height of 4,973 metres. This glacier, 12 kilometres long, covers an area of 38 square kilometres and is 300 metres in depth. An area of some 20,000 square kilometres is a zone of permafrost.

The republic has almost 85,000 rivers, of which 8,000 are over 10 kilometres long. The biggest is the Irtysh (4,248 kilometres), which flows through the territory of Kazakhstan for 1,400 kilometres. It rises on the western slope of the Mongol Altai, at a height of 2,500 metres, where it is called the Kara Ertys (Black Irtysh), but after passing through Lake Zaysan, it emerges under the name of Irtysh. Large hydro-electric power stations and the Irtysh-Karaganda Canal have been built on the river, which is 120 to 150 metres wide.

The River Ili, formed in the Tien Shan (Tien Mountains) by the confluence of two rivers, the Tekes and Kunges, is the main artery of Lake Balkhash. It has a total length of 1,439 kilometres, of which 802 are within the borders of Kazakhstan. The Ili flows through a broad valley, where it is 150 to 300 metres wide. Below the town of Kapchagay it spreads out on the Kapchagay plateau, where the Kapchagay hydro-electric station is located, and forms a huge artificial lake.

The Syr Darya (river), 2,212 kilometres in length, rises beyond the southern borders of Kazakhstan in the Tien Shan. Before emptying into the Aral Sea, this meandering river, which is salty in its lower course, forms numerous branches and channels, some of which peter out in the sands of the Kyzylkum (Red Desert).

Another major river, the Ural (2,534 kilometres), which has its source in the southern Ural Mountains, flows south for 1,084 kilometres through the western part of Kazakhstan, crossing a broad plain dotted with lakes. Before it enters the Caspian Sea, this mighty waterway, 500 metres wide in places, divides into many branches.

In northern Kazakhstan the main rivers, besides the Irtysh, are the Tobol and the Ishim. All three flow northward and in Russia join the River Ob on its way to the Arctic Ocean. In the central region, the Sary Su and Nura are typical winding rivers of the plains. Other important rivers are the Chu, which rises in Kirgizstan and eventually dries up through evaporation in the great Betpak-Dala salt basin, the Ayaguz, which drains into Lake Balkhash, the Emba, which empties into the Caspian, and the Ilek, Torgay, Irgiz and Talas. There are also many streams which flow only in the spring and dry up in summer.

The high mountain regions of Kazakhstan often suffer from destructive floods, which are especially frequent in the Zaili Alatau and Jungar Alatau. These are caused by the bursting of subterranean and surface bodies of water, natural reservoirs formed by heavy precipitation and the melting of snow and glaciers. Catastrophic floods, which carried off hundreds of lives and wreaked widespread devastation, have occurred over the years in the regions of Lesser and Greater Almatinka. Various engineering works to prevent flooding have been carried out on rivers that are flood hazards. In Lesser Almatinka, in the isolated Medeo mountain resort region, a flood disaster was averted in 1973 by the construction of a stone dam, 150 metres high and with a base of nearly 200 metres. This dam now securely protects the capital, Almaty, from flooding.

Lakes

The lakes of Kazakhstan, numbering almost 50,000, are scattered throughout the country. In some cases they are separated from each other by hundreds of kilometres, and in others, they are clustered close together to form lake districts. In the lowlands and desert regions they are mostly salty and many of them disappear in summer. Apart from Tengiz in central Kazakhstan, the biggest lakes are in the southern half of the country—Balkhash, Alakol and Sasykkol near the Jungar Pass, and Markakol in the Altai. In the south-western part of the republic are the largest salt lakes without outflow in the world: the Aral and Caspian seas.

The Aral Sea, called by the ancient Greeks the 'Scythian Gulf', is fed by two great rivers, the Amu Darya, which flows into its southern part in Uzbekistan, and the Syr Darya. Since the 1970s, however, intensive use of their waters, especially for irrigation of cotton fields, has drastically reduced the inflow into the sea, which is now shrinking at an alarming rate. The shores have already receded by 60 kilometres and more, and it is estimated that the Aral Sea could dry up completely within thirty years. The dry seabed has become incredibly salty, the level of underground waters has fallen sharply, the fishing industry has declined, the ecology of the islands and shores has suffered immense damage, and the productivity of arable land and pastures has decreased. In the northern part of the sea is the island of Barsakelmes, to which many species of animals and birds had been introduced: steppe antelopes, gazelles, wild asses, swans, pelicans, cormorants. Because of the deterioration of ecological conditions, the wildlife of the sanctuary has been moved to nature reserves in the Almaty and Taldy-Korgan provinces. The threat to the Aral Sea comes not only from drawing off the water that feeds it, but from a high degree of industrial and other chemical pollution, which has affected the health of many people living around its shores.

The Caspian Sea is, in fact, the biggest salt-water lake in the world, but is called a sea because of its size: it covers an area of 371,000 square kilometres and has a shoreline of 2,340 kilometres. It took its name from the tribe of Caspians who populated its shores in ancient times. The Caspian is a major oil region with a high concentration of oil and gas drilling works, gas conversion and chemical plants. The main ports of the Kazakhstan part are Aktau and Guryev. Oil, wood, grain, cotton and other goods are transported on the Caspian.

The sea is, of course, world-famous for its many types of sturgeon, the most important of which for their market value are the sterlet, white sturgeon, stellate sturgeon and beluga. The last can grow up to 1,000 kg. in weight. In the Volga and Ural rivers, sturgeon can weigh up to 80 kg. The Caspian fishing industry takes first place in the republic in the production of high-quality black caviar. Fish stocks in the sea have become somewhat depleted in recent years as a result of overfishing (mostly illegal poaching), pollution and oil exploration.

Thermal and mineral waters and industrial salts are abundant in Kazakhstan. The mineral springs, which have elements of hydrogen sulphide, chalybeate, bromide, iodine, radon and silica, are used for treatment in spa resorts and health centres. The underground thermal springs are potentially important sources of central heating and energy.

Flora and Fauna

Of the 6,500 plant species that grow in Kazakhstan, the majority are herbaceous, with relatively few varieties of bushes and trees. Plant life varies with the type of soil and climatic zones.

In the wooded and dry-steppe zones, conifers and grasses predominate. The semi-desert has a very limited range of plant life, whereas in the southern deserts this is surprisingly varied: small trees, saxaul (halaxylon) and other bushes grow in the sands. In the wooded steppe and the forest zone there are mixed deciduous and coniferous, walnut and maple forests. In the north of Kazakhstan and in the Tien Shan, pine predominates, in the Altai coniferous taiga can be found, while in the west there are beech, elm and poplar woods. Trees bearing edible nuts and fruit include pistachios, almonds, apples, apricots, plums and cherries. There is also an abundance of medicinal herbs and plants used for tanning.

Agricultural activities, including the ploughing up of the steppe, have significantly depleted the country's flora, so that nearly 300 rare plants are now protected by a special preservation order and are entered into the 'Red Book' of the republic.

The exceptionally varied fauna of Kazakhstan includes some very rare species of great scientific interest and many kinds of valued game animals and birds. There are 158 species of mammal, 485 different birds and almost 150 fish.

The desert and semi-desert zones are home to such creatures as gazelles, steppe antelopes, jerboas, lizards, snakes, and the poisonous karakurt and falang spiders. The Altai Mountains are inhabited by wild sheep, Siberian mountain goat, Siberian deer, wild goat, tundra partridge, wolverine and brown bear. The wildlife population of the Jungar Alatau and Tien Shan includes the snow leopard, the Himalayan mountain partridge, the Himalayan mountain finch and other rare species of wildlife. Common denizens of the wooded steppe are the white and grey hare, elk, wild goat, black grouse and white partridge; the wild turkey, gopher, lesser bustard and black skylark can be found on the open steppe.

Seven endangered species are the wild ass, cheetah, snow leopard, karakal sheep, gazelle, musk-rat and river beaver. Some seventy mammals are protected by preservation orders and are entered in the 'Red Book'.

Kazakhstan has many areas that can rightly be described as 'pearls of nature'. These include the enchanting lakes in the Kokshetau and Pavlodar regions and the amazing peaks of the Tien Shan, the unique wooded massifs of Karkaralinsk and Bayanaul in eastern Kazakhstan, and many other scenic areas that have retained their virginal beauty, wildlife and flora.

Six areas, Aksu-Jabaglin, Almaty, Korgaljin, Barsakelmes, Naurzum and Markakol, have been declared sanctuaries, to be preserved in their natural state. Their territory and waterways cannot be used for agriculture or any other activity that might disrupt the harmony of nature. The primary purpose of the sanctuaries is the preservation of nature and scientific research. The Aksu-Jabaglin, Almaty and Markakol sanctuaries are notable for the splendid mountain scenery of the Tien Shan and South Altai. The Naurzum sanctuary incorporates the southernmost pine woods in the steppe zone, Korgaljin the marshlands in the Tengiz-Korgaljin depression of central Kazakhstan, while Barsakelmes is an uninhabited island in the Aral Sea.

Kazakhstan's population, numbering over 17 million, is made up of more than a hundred nationalities, differing in language, culture and certain aspects of their everyday life, but closely connected by their shared history. The largest ethnic groups are the Kazakhs and the Russians, and the main religions, Islam and Christianity. The majority of the Kazakhs live in the arid western and southern regions and are engaged in agriculture and livestock farming. The Russian population of Kazakhstan and most of the other nationalities are concentrated in the north and east, and also in the industrial regions of the republic.

The Kazakh people, which includes many tribes in its ethnic make-up, is one of the oldest in Eurasia and played an important role in the history of the Eurasian steppe. A characteristic feature of the complex kin and tribal structure is the ethno-political groupation called a *juz* (horde or clan). During the period of their khanate, from the sixteenth to nineteenth century, the Kazakhs were divided into three *juz*: the Great Horde in eastern Kazakhstan, the Middle Horde in the central regions, and the Little Horde in the west. This division can be explained by historical causes and the existence of three natural, geographical regions. There is a theory that the hierarchy of the hordes was based on the order of seniority of the three sons of the legendary Alash, whose name is linked with the beginning of the independent existence of the Kazakhs.

The ethnogenesis of the Kazakhs extends as far back as the Bronze Age. The ancient inhabitants of present-day Kazakhstan were Indo-Iranian tribes of European physical type. The first written information about them and their dispersal on the territory of modern Kazakhstan refers to the Sak (Scythian) and Sarmatian tribes, which were close to each other in culture and spoke Eastern Iranian languages.

The large-scale penetration of Turkic peoples into the territory of Kazakhstan marked the beginning of an important new stage in the processes of ethnogenesis. In the period of its farthest expansion, the Turkic Empire of the sixth century occupied a huge area: Mongolia, vast areas of Siberia north of Lake Baikal and around the upper Yenisey, as far west as the Crimea, and to the upper reaches of the Amu Darya in the south. There was undoubtedly a genetic link amongst the early medieval population of Kazakhstan: the Turki, the Tyurgesh, the Karluks, the Oguz, the Karakhanids, the Kypchaks, the Naimans, the Kereits and other tribes who formed components of the Kazakh people.

The Kazakh ethnic community only really began to emerge when its members developed a sense of common identity arising out of the use of a single language and a shared system of moral values and culture. This ethnic consciousness is manifested by the single name they gave themselves: 'Kazakh', which began to be used in the latter half of the fifteenth century, when the Kazakh khanate was founded. The horde (*juz*) in many ways preserved the composition of the tribes and tribal unions of the past. The gradual evolution of the economy, changes in societal relations and the strengthening of early forms of feudalism all contributed to the formation of a single Kazakh nation and Kazakh statehood at this time.

The penetration of imperial Russia into the steppe, the setting up of capitalist production and the stream of settlers from Russia, which began in the sixteenth century, in the reign of Ivan IV, and swelled into a torrent after the abolition of serfdom, led to a sharp increase in the presence of other nationalities, as well as to the social stratification of the Kazakh aul (village). The census of 1897 recorded that 85 per cent of the population of the country were Kazakhs, and 12 per cent Russians and Ukrainians, with smaller numbers of Tatars, Uzbeks, Karakalpaks, Uygurs and Dungans.

The tsarist policy of colonization, harvest failure, and Russia's economic difficulties resulted in a further influx of Russian settlers in the 1890s. From the 1870s to 1890s, Uygurs and Dungans from Eastern Turkestan also settled in Kazakhstan.

In the years of revolution and civil war, the growth of the Kazakh population slowed down as a result of war losses, a low birth rate and high mortality.

In the first decades of Soviet power, the liquidation of the richer strata, harsh repression and famine all contributed to a decline in the Kazakh population. According to data on resettlement, in the first year of 'dispossession of *kulaks*' (1921), the number of wealthier farmers sent into exile from Kazakhstan amounted to 6,765. At the same time, the territory of Kazakhstan was prescribed by the Stalin administration as an area of '*kulak* exile' for many tens of thousands of better-off peasants from the Volga area, the central black earth province, from Central Asia and from beyond the Caucasus.

The most tragic result of the criminal Stalinist policy gambles was the famine of 1928 to 1931, in which 1.7 million of the Kazakh population perished. Nearly a million people moved out of Kazakhstan,

some to foreign countries—China, Iran, Afghanistan, Mongolia; of these, 600,000 did not return to the homeland. In 1937, 100,000 Koreans were resettled in Kazakhstan from the far eastern regions of the Soviet Union.

Over the first three or four decades of Soviet power, on the territory of Kazakhstan dozens of concentration camps were established, to which repressed peoples were exiled, together with criminals from all parts of the Soviet Union.

Just before and during the Great Patriotic War (1941-45), Kazakhstan accommodated 532,500 evacuees from the western borders of the Soviet Union—Russians, Jews, Latvians and others, 102,500 deported Poles, more than 361,000 deported Volga Germans, and 507,000 inhabitants of the North Caucasus—Chechens, Ingushes, Balkars, Karachais, Kalmyks, as well as Crimean Tatars, Turks, Kurds and Greeks. The Kazakhs, famous for their traditional hospitality, took them in and shared with them their last crust of bread. Many peoples of the Caucasus, remembering with gratitude the support they received in those terrible times, call Kazakhstan their second homeland.

Since Germany's reunification, the Germans in Kazakhstan, to everyone's regret, have been moving to their ethnic homeland. The warm fellow-feeling for them will long remain in the memories of the Kazakhs. Many of the Germans were educated in Kazakh schools, and had a brilliant command of the Kazakh language and deep appreciation of the literature and culture; they understood and loved the soul of the steppe people. The government is helping those who wish to leave, but it is also doing all it can to create conditions that will encourage the Germans to remain in the republic.

History has ordained that the Kazakhs should become a national minority in the land of their forefathers, but in view of the present high birth rate and the current emigration tendencies among other nationalities, they may again form the majority in the near future. It must be said that many ethnic Kazakhs have lost contact with the language, culture and religion of their forefathers: nowadays, more than 60 per cent speak and write only in Russian. The process of national revival will, it is hoped, encourage many people to re-evaluate the importance of the native language.

The growth of nationalism in Eastern Europe and in the former republics of the USSR, and the provocative acts of some political opportunists aimed at stirring up discord among the nationalities in Kazakhstan, have created a degree of concern. However, the consolidating policy of the President, the tolerance and loyalty of the native population, and the good relations built up over decades inspire confidence that social and political stability in the republic will be preserved. Another important cohesive factor is the large number of interethnic marriages over the years. In towns these represent 26.3 per cent of all marriages, and in rural areas 20.1 per cent.

The majority of people, 57 per cent to be precise, live in towns. The working population of the republic numbers 7.3 million. One of Kazakhstan's achievements is the high general level of education, the result of major investment in this field and of the intensive industrialization of the country. Children and young people up to the age of fifteen make up 31 per cent of the population. In 1992, half a million students enrolled at institutions of higher education. The solving of global problems of health and social welfare, which is closely interconnected with economic stability, is an important part of the state strategy.

48

*34. Children gaze in wonder at the
'eternal flame' that honours the memory
of all soldiers from Kazakhstan who died
in the Great Patriotic War (1941-45).*

35. Monument to 28 Kazakh soldiers of the 316th Infantry Division, under the command of Major General I. V. Panfilov, who heroically held up the advance of a large German tank unit in 1941, during the defence of Moscow in World War II.

*36. Kazakhs, Russians and many other
nationalities make up the armed forces of
Kazakhstan.*

37. *The colourful Republic Day festival is an event that delights young and old alike.*

38. The national holiday is an occasion
for the many different ethnic groups of
Kazakhstan to wear their traditional
costumes, which are kept for special
celebrations.

39. The elegance and exquisite workman-
ship of the traditional dress are shown to
particular advantage when worn by a
pretty girl.

40. A graceful Uygur girl performs one of her national dances at the Republic Day festival. The Uygur minority in Kazakhstan numbers about 150,000.

41. Members of a Korean dance group get ready for their performance in the festival. There are about 100,000 ethnic Koreans living in Kazakhstan.

42. In Almaty, as in other towns, young
people of various nationalities gather in
the evenings to dance, chat and show off
their finery.

43. Discotheques and parties provide opportunities for the young to meet, fall in love, and behave just like their contemporaries in the West.

44. *An attractive girl is never short of admirers. Young Kazakhs are no longer expected, as in the past, to marry their parents' choice of husband or wife.*

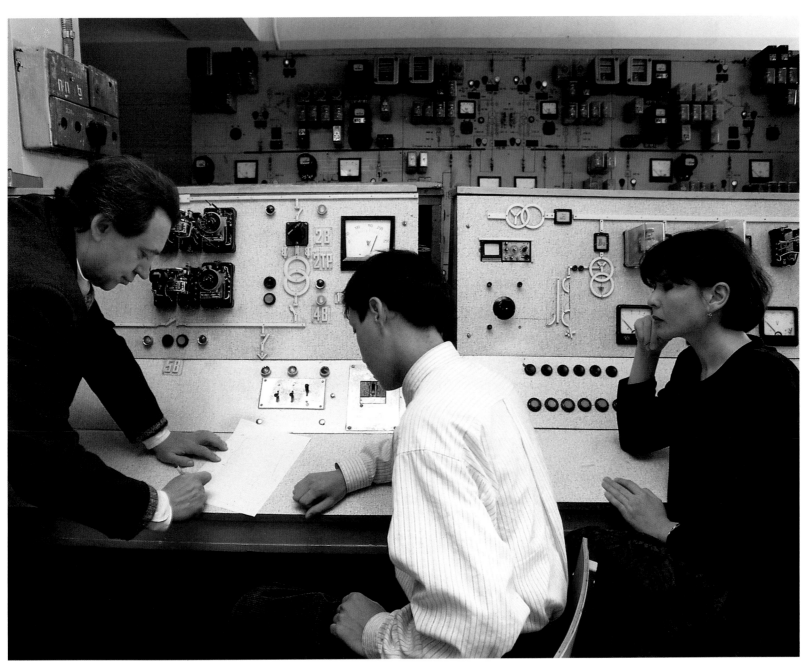

45. Young people from all regions study at the universities in Almaty. Practical work in the laboratory is a compulsory part of the study process.

46. Books are on sale not only in book-shops, but on almost every street corner in Almaty and other large towns. Reading remains a favourite pastime among townspeople, in spite of competition from television.

47. The circus is popular with all ages and among all sections of society in Kazakhstan. Despite their imposing size, the proud 'ships of the desert' are easily trained.

48. Almaty Circus, an impressive modern building with a huge dome, can seat over 2,000 spectators. The excellent permanent circus company has a repertoire with a pronounced national flavour.

52. The women and girls of Almaty love to skate in their free time. The long, cold winters give them plenty of opportunity to enjoy this sport.

53. When there are no official competitions at Medeo, the people of nearby Almaty can take advantage of its excellent facilities.

54. Winter with its frost and snow may make daily life more difficult for grown-ups, but it is always welcomed by the young. Childhood memories of games in the snow remain for a lifetime.

HISTORY

The Ancient World of Nomads

The early history of Kazakhstan is peopled by tribes of pastoralists who lived on the grassy expanses of the steppes between the Volga and the Altai Mountains in the third and second millennia BC. However, archaic stone tools, rock pictures and cave paintings similar to those found in Africa and South-east Asia indicate that the territory of southern Kazakhstan was inhabited by man as far back as the fourth millennium BC.

With the introduction of the wheeled cart from the Middle East in the third millennium BC, the Indo-European tribes began to migrate. Light battle chariots and horse harness were developed, and tools and weapons were improved. The broad expanses of Siberia, the Ural foothills, Kazakhstan and Central Asia were populated by tribes who left behind traces of a brilliant, original culture.

In the middle of the second millennium BC, the nomadic tribes inhabiting the territory of modern Kazakhstan made a discovery that marked the beginning of a new era: the technology of smelting bronze. The Bronze Age ushered in a more sedentary way of life based on agriculture as well as herding. Settlements surrounded by protective structures appeared, and there is evidence of a high level of building skill. Early forms of mining were developed to extract gold, copper and lead. The rich deposits of many metals in Kazakhstan and the beginning of the production of bronze had a significant impact on the tribes of the steppes. During this period, the intensive development of herding and metallurgy, which demanded hard physical labour, enhanced the social importance of the male. The communal clan lifestyle gradually gave way to smaller family units practising monogamy. Personal and then family property appeared, as is borne out by the *tagma*: a mark of personal ownership discovered on pottery vessels from around the beginning of the first millennium BC.

The Saks. Our information about the peoples who inhabited the territory of Kazakhstan in the first millennium BC comes primarily from Greek written sources, including Herodotus' *Histories*, based on Persian and Greek oral testimony, personal observation and some earlier writings, and also from the cuneiform rock inscriptions of the Achaemenid rulers. The inscriptions of the Persian Emperor Darius on the Bestukhin rock tell of a campaign against the 'Saks in their pointed caps'. The Persepolis inscription of Xerxes, the successor of Darius, makes reference to the tribal union of Saks as subject to the Persians. The Saks are also mentioned in the *Avesta*, the scriptures of the Zoroastrian religion of the ancient Iranians. In Persian written sources, the Eastern Iranian nomad tribes of Central Asia and Kazakhstan are called 'Turs with swift horses', who resisted the Aryan society of settled herders and farmers. The same eastern tribes that are called 'Saks' in the ancient Persian cuneiform texts are referred to in Greek works as 'Scythians', a name which became a synonym for the nomads.

In their accounts of the wars between the Saks and the Persians, Herodotus described the victory of the Saks over the Achaemenid emperor, Cyrus II, who had subjugated all the countries from Iran to the Mediterranean. In 539 BC, Cyrus II destroyed Babylon and was preparing to conquer Egypt, but the situation in the north-east of his domains, that is, Central Asia, prevented him from launching his Egyptian campaign. Instead, in order to secure his rear and destroy the powerful Central Asian nomads, Cyrus went to war with the Saks. But he did not count on the cunning of their fearless queen, Tomiris. After he had by deception annihilated a Sak force together with her son,

59. Future Olympic bob-sled champions, perhaps. Almaty has recently constructed a fine Olympic sports centre that is the pride of the city.

Tomiris responded with similar craftiness. She laid an ambush in the mountains by ordering her troops to flee and luring Cyrus and his army of 200,000 into a gorge. After the slaughter, there was not even a messenger left alive to tell the Persians of the terrible defeat. The Queen threw the Emperor's severed head into a leather bag full of human blood and passed sentence on his cruelty with these words: 'Be satiated now with the blood you thirsted for, and of which you could never have enough.' This is how a historian recounted the tale of the legendary queen and the 'mounted bowmen' who bravely defended their freedom.

One of the most renowned episodes in the history of the Saks is the unsuccessful attempt of Alexander of Macedon to subjugate them, whereby the warrior nomads checked the advance of the great conqueror to the east.

Archaeological finds—burial grounds, rock drawings, treasure troves—are the most important source of information on the formation of the society and culture of the Saks. On the banks of the rivers Talas, Chu and Ili, in the foothills of the Zaili and Jungar Alatau, and in the mountain valleys of Kegen and Narynkol, a large number of Sak burial grounds have been discovered, including royal burial vaults.

The burial mound at Issyk, some fifty kilometres from Almaty in the foothills of the Alatau, is an exceptionally rich site, dating from the sixth to fifth century BC. Here was discovered the burial vault of a Sak leader, whom archaeologists have called 'the gold man', as his clothes, armour and head-dress were decorated with some four thousand finely crafted disks and rectangles of gold. The central chamber of the tomb had been robbed in ancient times, but in a side chamber the body was found laid out on a cloth decorated with small gold disks. By the southern wall of the vault wooden dishes and vessels were found: four square dishes, a bucket and bowls. By the western wall there were pottery pitchers and bowls, a silver spoon with a handle in the form of a heron, a silver cup with an eight-petalled rosette on the bottom, and a miniature silver ritual cup with a two-line inscription of 26 characters, similar to runic script, which has not yet been deciphered. By the left hand of the deceased lay an arrow with a gilded shaft and a gold tip, and a whip with a gold ribbon round the handle; in a leather toilet bag there was a bronze mirror and a small piece of ochre.

The dead leader was dressed in a red suede jacket covered with small gold triangles, imitating armour. His leather trousers, decorated with a border of gold disks, were tucked into boots which had gold triangles sewn along the tops. The figure was crowned by a tall leather cap with gold ornamentation depicting wild animals and birds, feathers, arrows, and mountains with trees on which birds were perched. The top of the cap was decorated with a tiny figure of a mountain sheep: an *arkhara*.

On the right-hand side of the body lay a long iron sword, sickle-shaped at the top, sheathed in a red wooden scabbard attached to a belt. On the left hung a dagger: an *akinak*. A ring, engraved with the head of a man in profile with a fine head-dress, was also discovered.

The culture, world-view and religion of the Saks is reflected in their art, with its realistic depiction of animals, people with faces like suns, chariots, battle scenes and ritual objects. Their flourishing bronze-age culture owed much to their contacts through trade with the cultures of the Mediterranean and Asia Minor.

Significant alliances were formed with the Kushan, Parthian, Sogdian and Chinese empires, and written evidence indicates that the

Sak tribes were on the threshold of statehood. The Usuns and Kangyus were the direct heirs of the Sak traditions.

The Usuns. The Usuns are one of the first peoples on the territory of Kazakhstan who had social class stratification. They came from the heart of Central Asia to the Jeti Su (Seven Rivers or Semi-rech'e) region in the south of Kazakhstan and inherited the lands of the Saks. The central territory of the Usuns was located in the Ili valley. In the west they bordered on the Kangyus, and in the east, the Huns. Chiguchen, the capital of the Usuns, was on the shore of Lake Issyk.

The Usuns' ethnic origin is still a subject of debate. Some researchers believe they were Irano-Persian tribes, while others consider them to have been the predecessors of the Turki. The name Usun, it may be noted, is borne by one of the most important Kazakh tribes.

The Usuns exploited the deposits of copper, lead, tin and gold and knew how to smelt iron, from which they made knives, swords, and arrow-heads. Usun society achieved the level of statehood.

The Kangyus. Mentioned in written sources dating from the second century BC, the Kangyus developed a powerful state in southern Kazakhstan at the beginning of the first millennium AD, which strove to control the section of the Great Silk Road from Fergana to near the Aral Sea. It played a not insignificant role in the history of the region and had political, economic and cultural ties with China, Parthia, Rome and the Kushan Empire.

Sources indicate that Kangyu covered an extensive territory, and was mainly populated by nomad tribes, though it also had towns. It was centred on the middle course of the Syr Darya, but its power extended to the northern shores of the Caspian. There is still no clear evidence of what language the Kangyus spoke. Some scholars think that they were a Turkic-speaking people; others take the view that they belonged to a group of northern Iranian pastoral tribes or were the descendants of Iranian-speaking Saks. In the regions where the Kangyus once held sway, archaeologists have discovered a large number of monuments.

The Huns. The reputation of this vanished people as being warlike and barbarous has survived to the present day. This is not surprising since under their leader, Attila, they swept through Europe, leaving devastation in their wake, and precipitated the fall of the Roman Empire. Pressure from the Huns was also responsible for the mass westward migration of peoples that plunged Europe into the Dark Ages. As the Huns advanced westward, they penetrated into the area round the Aral Sea and western Kazakhstan. For a time, the lands under the control of the Huns stretched from the area beyond Baikal to Tibet and from Eastern Turkestan to the middle flow of the Khuankhe River. In the fourth century, together with other nomadic tribes, they reached the southern Russian steppes and the Danube.

The Huns were the forerunners of the Turkic people and their penetration into Kazakhstan is linked to the Turkicizing of the Eastern Iranian tribes of the Kangyus. Herding played an important part in the life of the Huns, but they are better remembered for their military prowess. Swift and manoeuvrable horsemen armed with bows and arrows made up the main body of their army. Written sources tell us of the existence among the Huns of private property in the form of cattle and land. This, together with the introduction of taxes and the spread of literacy, marked further progress towards the evolution of a class-based society and state in these regions.

The Turkic Tribes

The middle of the sixth century brought Turkic tribes to the territory of Kazakhstan, and the rise of an early feudal state, the Turkic kaganate. Founded in 551, it established its hegemony over Central Asia and maintained political and economic ties with the most important states of that time: Byzantium, Sassanid Iran and China. It waged a war for control of the Great Silk Road linking China with the Mediterranean. In 603 the kaganate split into two independent states: eastern and western.

From 630 to 682 the Eastern Turkic kaganate, which had occupied Mongolia, was very weak, but following a protracted struggle with China (679-87) it reasserted its independence. The first kagan was Kutlug, and his closest aid and adviser a man named Tonykok, who left an account of his actions inscribed on a stone stele in the ancient Turkic runic script. The kaganate became especially powerful under Kapan (691-716). After his death, Bilge and his brother Kyul-Tegin came to power. The last information about the Eastern Turki in Chinese sources dates from 914: at this period part of the Turki were among the tribes who formed the state of the Karakhanids.

The Western Turkic kaganate occupied the territory from the slopes of the Karatau to Jungaria and part of Eastern Turkestan. Istemi, the founder of the Western Turkic kaganate, bore the name of Yabgu, which was traditional for the western branch of the Turkic dynasty. In 558, the Turki subjugated the area round the Volga and the Ural foothills, including the Bolgar Turkic tribes living there. From 561 to 563 the Turki waged war against the Aftalites, who ruled over Central Asia and Afghanistan. After the conquest of Central Asia, the Turki became masters of the Great Silk Road.

The Western Turkic kaganate differed significantly from the Eastern in that most of its population were settled, engaged in arable farming, crafts and trade. A significant role in the formation of the early medieval urban and agrarian culture of the Western Turkic kaganate was also played by the Sogdians, Syrians and Persians, who inhabited the bigger towns. They founded Christian, Manichaean, Zoroastrian and Buddhist religious communities that had a cultural and ideological influence on the Turkic population. As a result of their missionary activity among the Turki, along with the Turkic runic writing on stone, Sogdian, Syrian and Manichaean inscriptions can be found.

Internecine struggles in the kaganate, the political actions of the Chinese Empire, which was trying to take over the lands of the Jeti Su, a succession of harvest failures due to bad weather and the resulting famines all contributed to the weakening of the kaganate's power which enabled the Tyurgesh tribe to gain control. In 756 the Tyurgesh kaganate fell in its turn, under the pressure of the Turkic Karluk tribe.

The Karluks moved in from the lands that lay towards the western Altai and seized power in the Jeti Su, forming an early feudal state (766-940). In the eighth to tenth century they lived in the territory between lakes Balkhash and Issyk, in the valleys of the rivers Ili, Chu and Talas. Though the Karluks' attempts to rival the Uygur kaganate were unsuccessful, they were powerful enough to check the penetration of the Arabs into Kazakhstan and supported revolts against the Arabs in Central Asia. The threat to the Karluk kaganate came from the direction of Eastern Turkestan, from pagan Turkic peoples. In 940 the Karluk state fell and the Karakhanids seized power.

The Oguz. The history of the Oguz is closely linked with the ter-

ritory of Kazakhstan. In the ninth century the Oguz tribes, united with the Khazar kaganate, held sway over the steppes in the region of the Aral Sea and in western Kazakhstan. The Oguz state played an important role in the political and military history of Eurasia. Its leader, Jabgu, allied himself with Prince Svyatoslav of Kievan Rus against the Khazars and in 965 their combined forces crushed the Khazar kaganate. At the end of the tenth century, in alliance with Vladimir, another prince of Kievan Rus, they destroyed the state of the Volga Bolgars. The Oguz state was remarkable for its multi-ethnic character, and for this very reason it never developed into a unified nation.

The eleventh century saw the decline of the Oguz state, which was overrun by the Turkic tribe of Kypchaks from the eastern steppe. Under pressure from the Kypchaks, large groups of Oguz migrated to the borders of Eastern Europe and to Asia Minor. Those who remained came under the rule of the Karakhanid state on the territory of Kazakhstan and Central Asia, and of the Turkic Seljuks in Iran. The remaining Oguz were assimilated in the eleventh century by the Turkic-speaking tribes of the Kypchak country: Desht-i-Kypchak.

The Arab Conquest. In 633 the Arabs began their campaigns of conquest under the banner of a Holy War. In an astonishingly short time they overran the territories of Iran, Syria, Palestine, Egypt and Iraq, and reached the southern provinces of Central Asia.

In 712 and 713, the Tyurgesh kaganate and the Central Asian states combined forces against the Arabs and heavily defeated them. But the subsequent weakening of the Tyurgesh kaganate allowed the Arabs to subjugate a series of provinces in Central Asia and the south of Kazakhstan. At this time Arab supremacy extended only to parts of southern Kazakhstan and the Jeti Su—their most notable conquests occurred only in the tenth to twelfth century.

The Arab invasion left its mark on the socio-economic, political and cultural life of the territories under the caliphate. The most significant change was the spread of the new state religion, Islam, and of Arabic language and literature. Gradually the old Turkic literature was replaced, and Arabic words entered the Turkic vocabulary. The predominance of Arabic literature led to the adoption of the language by many outstanding scholars and poets. Ispidjab, Otrar, Taraz and other towns became important centres of culture where great scholars and poets, such as al-Farabi, al-Buruni and Abu Ali ibn-Sina, lived and worked.

Karakhanids and Karakhitais. The state of the Karakhanids (940-1212), which included within its boundaries the provinces of Kashgar and Jeti Su, was the first Muslim feudal state in this region. The Karakhanid dynasty's acceptance of Islam had an immense influence on the Turkic tribes. This was a period of intensive settlement of the Turkic nomads, resulting in profound changes in the system of economic and social relations, the growth of towns and development of material culture. In 960 the Karakhanids proclaimed Islam as the state religion. At the same time the Arabic script was adopted, ousting the ancient Turkic alphabet. Nevertheless, important literary works were written in the Turkic language and Turkic architectural monuments were built.

At the end of the eleventh and beginning of the twelfth century, the political situation in the steppe became unstable as the Karakhanid state fell into decline and began to split into separate feudal domains. The invasion of Kazakhstan by the Mongol Karakhitais (Khitans)

85

around 1130 eventually led to the fall of the Karakhanids.

In the middle of the twelfth century, the realm of the Karakhitais incorporated the expanses of Kazakhstan, Bukhara, Samarkand and the state of Mawarannahr. The borders of the realm were not stable, but the conquered lands stretched from the Tien Shan to Khorezm. In 1206, under pressure from Chingis Khan, Kuchluk Khan, the leader of the Naimans, left the Altai for the Jeti Su area. At that time the vassals of the Karakhitai ruler in this area rose against him. Taking advantage of this, Kuchluk Khan formed an alliance of the Naimans and Kireits, captured the leader of the Karakhitais and seized power in the Jeti Su area. (The nomadic Naimans and Kireits were to become ethnic components in the Kazakh nation.)

The Kypchaks. Early in the eleventh century, the allied Kypchak tribes succeeded the ethno-political unions that had previously controlled this territory. Like their predecessors—the Saks, Huns, Turki, Tyurgesh, Karluks, Oguz—the Kypchaks were mostly nomadic pastoralists, though they also had settled farming communities. Trade developed, based on the value of exchange of livestock until the use of money was introduced.

The Kypchaks' external political connections were wide-ranging, extending to Byzantium, Kievan Rus, Georgia, the Seljuk sultanate, Volga Bolgaria and Hungary. They also had close contacts with the peoples and civilizations of Asia and the Far East.

The Age of Mongol Expansion

The beginning of the thirteenth century saw the founding of the powerful empire of Chingis (Genghiz) Khan, who united several Mongol groups under his leadership. He succeeded in stopping inter-tribal wars and reconciling the leaders by the prospect of external conquest with its opportunities for enrichment by plunder and the acquisition of fertile farm lands.

One of the reasons for the military success of Chingis Khan was the alliance with the military forces of the Turkic tribes of Central Asia and Kazakhstan. The Turkic tradition was a dominant influence in the formation of the Mongol state. Chingis Khan's military organization was based on the Turkic kaganate's system, in which the troops of the nomad communities were divided into tens, hundreds, thousands and tens of thousands. The empire of Chingis Khan took on board these administrative units.

The first main campaign of the Horde of Chingis Khan was directed against the territory of Kazakhstan and Central Asia. The ambitious conqueror had already set his sights on Eastern Europe and the Near East, and for this reason took a long time in painstakingly preparing the campaign against Kazakhstan. From Muslim merchants and various deserters he gathered reliable information about the internal situation and military strength of the Karakhanids and the shah of Khorezm. His plan of campaign was well thought out and efficiently executed.

In 1212 Chingis defeated the Naimans and beheaded their leader, Kuchluk, thus opening up the way to southern Kazakhstan and Central Asia. The Mongols encountered the first resolute opposition at the gates of the city of Otrar, the cultural centre of southern Kazakhstan. The six-month-long siege of the city ended in February 1220, when the last warriors laid down their lives and its ruler, Gayir, was captured and cruelly executed. The city was then mercilessly wiped off the face of the earth, an event known in history as the Otrar catastrophe.

All the towns of the Syr Darya region resisted heroically, as did the Kypchaks of western Kazakhstan, who were defeated in a bloody battle. Muslim writers of the thirteenth century have left a full account of these events. The Mongol conquest scattered Kypchaks throughout many countries, though the core population remained in their homeland. In 1241 a group headed by Kotyan fled to Hungary, where they were taken into the king's service. Others fled north to Volga Bolgaria. At the end of the thirteenth century many fugitive Kypchaks appeared in the Russian lands, Romania, Poland and Lithuania. Kypchaks who were taken captive by the Mongols were sold into slavery to Europe, north-west Africa, and very many of them to Egypt and India.

The Kypchak young men, like the Turki in general, were highly valued as warriors: as Mamelukes (soldier slaves) they formed the personal guards of the Muslim rulers of Egypt and India. History records the names of steppe Kypchaks who when serving as Mamelukes and Gulyams (house slaves) rose to the most surprising heights of power.

In 1250 the Kypchak Mamelukes seized power in Egypt, to which many slaves of Turkic origin had been sold. The Mameluke guard was the military force that blocked the progress of the Mongol conquerors, who had never before known defeat. They thus saved Cairo from the fate that had befallen Baghdad and Damascus, where, according to chroniclers, at the time of the invasion 'blood flowed in the streets like a river'.

Egypt and Syria, the centres of Muslim civilization, were surrounded by enemies: from the east the Mongols and from the west the European Crusaders. The Kypchak Mamelukes repulsed both threats.

In 1260, Muzzafar Qutuz, the Mameluke ruler, inflicted a crushing defeat on the Mongols in Syria. His successor, Baibars I, who ruled Egypt for seventeen years, was famous not only on the battlefield, but as a wise statesman who ensured the country's economic prosperity. El-Markizi gives evidence that Baibars was born in the Kypchak steppes.

A new dynasty that was to govern Egypt for one hundred and three years came to power in 1280. Its founder was the Mameluke Sultan Qalaun (Kalavan), who was also born in Desht-i-Kypchak. His son, Mohammad el-Nasir I, ruled Egypt for most of the next forty-two years, to be succeeded by nine of his sons in turn. In 1382 this dynasty was replaced by the Burji (Circassian) Mamelukes, who held the throne down to 1517, when Egypt became part of the immense Ottoman Empire.

Outstanding monuments of Islamic architecture have survived in Egypt from the Kypchak Mameluke era. One of the most beautiful architectural ensembles in Cairo, comprising a mosque, mausoleum and hospital, was built by Sultan Qalaun (1284-85). El-Nasir's rule was likewise notable for the construction of religious buildings which survive to this day. In the thirteenth and fourteenth centuries, Egypt attracted many Muslim scholars, philosophers, craftsmen and teachers, whose safety was guaranteed by the powerful Mameluke sultanate. The flourishing of culture, science and art in Egypt was thus made possible through the bravery and military skill of the Mamelukes, the Turkic warriors from Desht-i-Kypchak, who saved Arab Muslim civilization from destruction.

The Kypchaks played an analogous role in India. In 1206 the Delhi

60. The monument to Abai, the great Kazakh poet, philosopher and composer, which stands on the busiest street of the capital.

sultanate was founded by the Kypchak gulyam Kutl-ad-Aybek, who was succeeded by Iltutmysh, a Kypchak from the Olburluk tribe. Unusually in the history of Muslim states at that time, Ruzaia, the daughter of Iltutmysh, then ascended the throne. From this it can be seen that, in accordance with the steppe tradition, women occupied a prominent place in society. Another notable Kypchak from the Olburluk tribe was Giyas-ad-din Balban, a famous commander in Delhi, who took the title Ulug Khan and ruled from 1226 to 1287.

After the disintegration of Chingis Khan's empire, the most important positions in the Mongol realms were occupied by Turki, who played a decisive role in the wars waged by Kublai Khan against the Chingisites and in the conquest of the Chinese Empire. The Kypchak Yantimur rose to the heights of power and ruled China from 1328 to 1333. Many poets, scholars, writers and artists of Turkic origin made an outstanding contribution to Chinese and Mongol culture of the thirteenth and fourteenth centuries.

Thus, the Kypchaks of medieval Kazakhstan and Eastern Europe, driven from their homeland steppes by the Mongol conquerors and sold into slavery, became the rulers of powerful, rich and highly civilized countries of the East and a major force in world politics of the thirteenth and fourteenth centuries. Indeed, mankind owes a great debt to the Kypchaks for saving the Arab and Indian civilizations from destruction.

The Mongol conquest was a massive disaster for Kazakhstan, as it was for other countries they overran. It had a profoundly retrogressive effect on the economic, political and cultural development of the population, provoked disunity among the local tribes, and led to the division of the settled population of the south and south-east farming regions. The large towns of Otrar, Sauran, Sygnak, Jent and others disappeared from the face of the earth.

At the time of the Mongol conquest, feudal relations in the settled regions of Kazakhstan had reached a high level of development, whereas in Mongolia such relations had scarcely been conceived of. The conquerors were at a lower level of social development than the local population. The Mongol invasion severely damaged the economy, destroyed the territorial and political integrity, and slowed down the formation of the Kazakh national identity, though it could not stop it, for the Turkic tribes preserved their customs and language.

The gigantic empire founded by fire and the sword was divided up among the sons of Chingis Khan: Juchi, Chagatay and Ugedey. In the fifth decade of the thirteenth century, the Golden Horde state was founded by Batu, the son of Juchi. The power of the khans of the Golden Horde extended over the territory from the lower Danube and Gulf of Finland in the west, to the Irtysh River and the lower Ob in the east, from the Black, Caspian and Aral seas and Lake Balkhash in the south, to the Novgorod lands in the north. The unstable nature of the state union, founded by force of arms, was aggravated by internecine strife and the struggle for liberation of the indigenous peoples, which led to the gradual weakening and eventual collapse of the Golden Horde. Khan Mamay's attempts to strengthen its position by plundering campaigns against the Russian principalities led to the heavy defeat of the Golden Horde by a combined Russian force at the battle of Kulikovo (1380). Another famous Mongol conqueror, Timur (Tamerlane), who aimed to recreate the empire of Chingis Khan, then swept from the east and in 1391 and 1395 finally destroyed the Golden Horde.

61. View of Almaty by night (overleaf). This attractive, modern city has nearly 1.2 million inhabitants. Known as the garden city, it is noted for its apples, from which it gained its name ('alma' means apple in Kazakh).

*62. The building of the Supreme Soviet
of the Republic of Kazakhstan.*

*63. The 'White House' of Kazakhstan,
the official residence of the President,
which was completed in 1994.*

64. Monument to Gani Muratbaev, the first Kazakh Komsomol (Communist Youth League member), in front of the Pioneers' Palace, a centre of entertainment, educational and cultural activities for the schoolchildren of Almaty.

65. In recent years some outstanding examples of modern architecture have embellished the capital. One such is the Hotel Kazakhstan, built in the late 1970s.

66. *Almaty railway station is an important link on the Trans-Siberian Railway network, which connects the capital with major industrial centres.*

67. *The building of the Academy of Sciences of Kazakhstan in Almaty, constructed in the 1950s, soon after the foundation of the Academy.*

68. *The Glory Memorial, the largest of a number of monuments in the central park of the capital that commemorate those who fell in the Great Patriotic War.*

69. *Monument in Semipalatinsk to the eminent Kazakh scholar Chokan Valikhanov and the great Russian writer Fyodor Dostoyevsky, who were friends for many years.*

*70. The dome of the large modern
building that houses Almaty Circus, with
a sculpture of a clown in the foreground.*

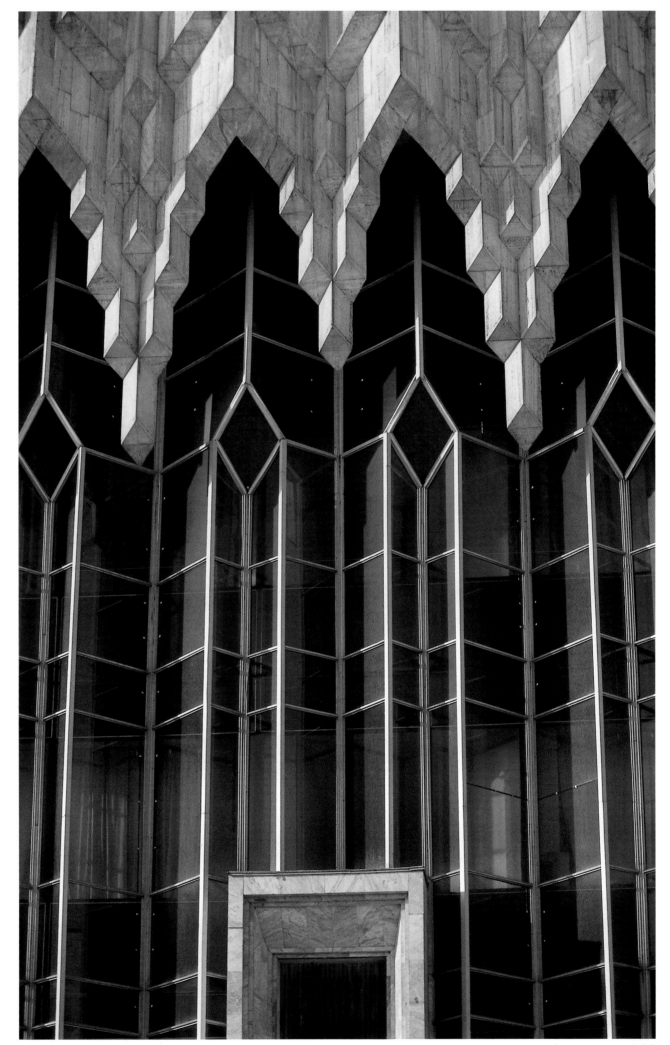

71, 72. Almaty has many modern buildings which successfully incorporate elements of old Kazakh, Central Asian and Arabian architecture.

101

73, 74. Almaty displays a great variety of architectural styles. This building dating from the 1930s has some unusual features reminiscent of early Russian buildings.

75, 76. This ornate nineteenth-century mercantile building in the capital was formerly used for both trade and the manufacture of cloth. It now houses a store selling textiles.

77, 78. This colourful old building with elaborate wood-carving attracts the attention of all visitors to Almaty. Quite appropriately, in view of its architectural merit, it now accommodates the Ministry of Culture.

79. *The new building of the Arasan City Baths in Almaty, which offers Turkish, Russian and Finnish baths and treatment with therapeutic mud.*

80. *The National Museum of Kazakhstan, built and opened in the late 1980s. The museum has a fascinating collection of archaeological, historical and ethnographic exhibits.*

81. *A feature of many towns in Kazakhstan is the juxtaposition of ancient and modern architecture. The old building here in Almaty houses the Museum of Musical Instruments.*

82. The main square of the city of Akmola, capital of Akmola province in the north of Kazakhstan. There are plans to move the state capital from Almaty to this city.

83. *An old street in Akmola from the time of imperial Russian rule. The city, which has 288,000 inhabitants, was known for a time as Tselinograd, until its old name was restored in 1992.*

84. *The Hotel Ishim in Akmola, named after the main river of Akmola province, which flows through the city.*

85. The style of urban architecture widespread in the Soviet Union can be seen in the city of Semipalatinsk, in the northeast of the country. The city is also known by its Kazakh name—Semey.

The united tribes of nomads who lived in the thirteenth to fifteenth centuries in what is now south and south-east Kazakhstan were known as the White Horde, and at first formed part of the realm of Juchi. In the fourteenth century this feudal union significantly developed and gained strength under Urus Khan and Tokhtomysh. In the period from 1428, Khan Abu'l Khayr ruled the White Horde. During Janibek's reign, in the sixth decade of the fifteenth century, the White Horde became the political basis of the Kazakh community.

In the middle of the fourteenth century, on the territory of south-east Kazakhstan and Kirgizia the feudal state of Mughulistan arose as a result of the collapse and division of the Chagatay Empire (named after Chagatay, the second son of Chingis Khan), which was formed by the Mongols in Central Asia. In its western domains, Mawarannahr, the Chagatay clan lost its predominance and power fell into the hands of Turkic-Mongol emirs, the most notable of whom was Timur (1370-1405), who came from the Turkicized Mongol Beybars tribe. In the eastern part, the khans of the Chagatay clan held sway. The nomads of the eastern part called themselves Mughuls, hence the name Mughulistan. Its attempts to subjugate Mawarannahr, internal strife and Timur's interference in the internal affairs of Mughulistan weakened the state, which was now confronted by an external threat.

The frequent raids by Timur on Mughulistan toward the end of the fourteenth century were accompanied by terrible atrocities and had disastrous consequences: the population was decimated, the process of ethno-political consolidation of the tribes of Kazakhstan and Kirgizia was retarded, the settled farming economies declined, and the number of livestock decreased.

The fall of the Golden Horde and the revival of the trade and economic centres after the destruction caused by the Mongol invasions contributed significantly to the creation of the Kazakh khanate.

The Kazakh Khanate

The formation of the khanate was the natural outcome of the social, economic and ethno-political processes that evolved on the territory of Kazakhstan in the fourteenth to fifteenth century. The gradual recovery from the Mongol conquest, the growing influence of the local Turkic nobles, and especially the intensified struggle of the population against the oppression of the Mongol khans and feudal powers, all worked towards political consolidation and the attainment of statehood on an ethnic basis. The khanate incorporated states that arose in the first half of the fourteenth century: Desht-i-Kypchak, the Ak Horde in Turkestan, the khanate of Abu'l Khayr—the Nogai Horde, and in the Jeti Su area—Mughulistan.

Many factors contributed to the formation of the Kazakh national identity in this period: the strengthening of feudal relations, the revival of agriculture and the cities in the south of Kazakhstan, and the growth of economic activity and trade. All this resulted in closer links between the nomadic and semi-nomadic peoples of the central steppe and the settled faming commuties of the Jeti Su, who were related by origin, language and culture. Towards the middle of the fifteenth century the need was felt for a stable union which could safeguard the national identity and economic activity of the Kazakhs. This accorded with the interests and wishes of the population at large: the nomad herders and the farmers in the oases of southern and eastern

94. The railway station in Akmola. Traditional Kazakh decorative elements are often used by modern architects to give a national stamp to their work.

Kazakhstan, who had suffered cruelly from the feudal oppression and strife that disrupted their lives and work. At the same time, the feudal lords also needed a powerful state that could protect their interests.

Instrumental in the formation of a united Kazakh khanate was the migration of some Kazakh clans and tribes of central and southern Kazakhstan to the Jeti Su area in the middle of the fifteenth century, in order to escape the rule of Khan Abu'l Khayr. In medieval times, moving out of a territory ruled by a khan was a widespread form of protest by the 'working class', the nomadic herders, against exploitation and oppression. Cleverly taking advantage of the people's discontent in their struggle for power, the far-sighted descendants of Khan Urus of the Ak Horde, the Chingisite sultans Janibek and Kerey, led the Kazakhs out of the territories of Khan Abu'l Khayr. In the Jeti Su area the Kazakh sultans entered into an alliance with Khan Esen Buga of Mughulistan, who was looking for support in his struggle against his brother, Yunus, a contender for power in Mughulistan, and at the same time striving to protect his borders from Abu'l Khayr, the Timurids and the Kalmyk leaders. After the death of Esen-Buga, the Kazakh sultans succeeded in founding an independent political union in the Jeti Su area—the Kazakh khanate. The author of *Tarihi-i-Rashidi*, Muhammad Haydar Doglati, names the year 470 of the Muslim calendar (i.e. 1465-66) as the date of its foundation.

The Kazakh khanate at first covered the territory of the western Jeti Su: the valleys of the rivers Chu and Talas, and subsequently united all the clans and tribes of central and southern Kazakhstan. After the death of Khan Abulkhair in 1468 during a campaign in the Jeti Su area, the Kazakh khans engaged in a struggle with various descendants of the Zhuchids for power in eastern Desht-i-Kypchak and Kokanda. Towards the end of the fifteenth century, Janibek, Kerey and Sultan Kasym succeeded in strengthening their control over a significant part of the territory settled by the Kazakh clans and tribes in Sarys and Syr Darya, in the area round the Aral Sea and the foothills of Karatau. Muhammad Shaibani, grandson of Abulkhair, who had conquered large area of Central Asia in the first decade of the sixteenth century, put up a stubborn struggle for the Syr Darya towns of Sygnak, Sauran, Otrar and Yasy, which were important administrative, political and trading points. The outcome was that Sauran, Suzak and Sygnak were included in the Kazakh khanate and Muhammad Shaibani was forced to leave for Mawarannahr, which he succeeded in taking from the Timurids.

In the sixteenth and seventeenth centuries the Kazakh khanate grew stronger and incorporated the greater part of the territory inhabited by the Kazakhs. It fostered ties with Central Asia, the khanates of Astrakhan, Kazan and Siberia, and the Russian state. The Kazakh khanate reached its zenith in the early sixteenth century under the rule of Kasym Khan, who rapidly expanded its borders and united the tribes. His victory in 1510 over the Central Asian leader Muhammad Shaibani put into his hands most of the towns of Turkestan, including Tashkent. The majority of these remained within the khanate for one and a half centuries. In the seventeenth century and the beginning of the eighteenth, these towns were its political centres, where the rulers resided. In the second decade of the sixteenth century, Kasym Khan finally established his control over the vast Kazakh lands. The borders of the khanate now reached as far as the Ural River.

After Kasym's death, his son, Hak Nazar Khan, vigorously continued the policy of his father, trying to consolidate and strengthen the

Kazakh khanate. But internal and external troubles thwarted his efforts to create a centralized Kazakh state on a lasting basis, for the hordes failed to establish firm political and economic ties.

The strong rule of Tauke Khan (1680-1718) saw the temporary strengthening of Kazakh statehood. He was one of the instigators of a legal code, the *Jeti Jargy*, which laid down the basic principles of feudal law and state organization. However, early in the eighteenth century the hordes again split into independent khanates with their own rulers. In this period the Kazakh realms, disunited and weakened by the internal struggle for power and separatism of the leaders, were confronted by grave external threats. The Volga Kalmyks made raids from the west, supported by the Yaitsky Cossacks; from the north the Siberian Cossacks attacked; the Bashkirs, who were subjects of the Russian Empire, laid claim to the nomad territory beyond the River Yaik; from the south the Central Asian khans applied pressure. But the greatest peril was from the south-east, from the strong and aggressive military-feudal Jungarian khanate.

The Jungar attacks on Kazakhstan had begun back in the fifteenth century, but at the end of the sixteenth they were defeated by the Kazakhs and became vassals of Khan Tevvekel. However, in the first half of the eighteenth century, the Kazakhs were unable to withstand the predatory ambitions of the Jungar leaders. In this period, which has entered their history as the Years of Disasters, they suffered enormous human and material losses that gravely destabilized economic and political life for a long time.

The critical situation facing the Kazakhs finally impelled them to unite and in 1758 their combined forces inflicted a crushing defeat on the Jungars, who thereafter disappeared from history. The leaders and heroes of the war of liberation were the knights (*batyrs*) Bugenbay, Kabanbay, Taylak, Janbek, Malaysary, Khan Abu'l Khayr, Abylay Khan and Semeke. The Jungar invasion, however, left deep scars on Kazakh society.

Relations at this time between the Kazakhs and the Russian subjects—the Ural Cossacks, the Kalmyks and Bashkirs—became more complicated. Peace on the western and northern frontiers became one of the main priorities of the Kazakh khanates, threatened as they were from the south and east by archaic and aggressive states: the Bukhara and Khiva khanates and Jungaria. The Kazakhs thus needed an alliance with the powerful northern neighbour, the Russian Empire. But through this alliance they gradually came under Russian control: the Little Horde in 1730 and later the territories of the Middle and Great hordes. By the middle of the following century, all of Kazakhstan had become a colony of the Russian Empire.

In the period of the Kazakh khanate, society was divided into two basic social groups. The upper rung of the social hierarchy was occupied by the aristocrats—*ak suek (*white bone), the sultans who were members of the dynasty of Chingis Khan (the Chingisites), and the hodjas, the missionaries of Islam who were descendants of close associates of the Prophet Muhammad. The term 'sultan', meaning wielder of power, was first used by the Seljuks in inscriptions on coins. The title of sultan was inherited by children of the Chingisites and the right to ascend the throne of the khan was reserved for the Chingisite sultans. Just below them in the hierarchy were the *tore*, who included the non-ruling Chingisites and the clan nobles.

The lower social stratum, the *kara suek* (black bone), was made up of the nomadic livestock herders united into clan communities, and slaves. Of the social group of the *kara suek*, only the *biis*—the local leaders—had special rights. Local judicial, administrative and military matters were in the hands of the *biis*, who were respected members of the community chosen by the people and confirmed by the khan.

There was also a division of the population according to property into beys (the rich) and *kedeys* (the poor), which was unconnected with membership of a social order. Though the richest beys were extremely influential in society, their wealth did not automatically confer special political rights. Any sultan, even one enjoying full rights and privileges, could become either a bey or a *kedey*.

Under the Russian Crown

On 10 October 1730, Abu'l Khayr, the khan of the Little Horde, signed an act whereby his territory in effect came under the rule of Russia. Lands that had been Kazakh from time immemorial were gradually annexed to the Russian Empire, and the Cossack military colonization commenced.

At the beginning of the eighteenth century, Peter I had defined the basic direction of imperial policy in relation to Central Asia and the Kazakh steppes. Peter considered Kazakhstan to be the 'key to the gates to all the Asian countries and lands'. The tsarist government began to strengthen its position and influence on the steppe, building towns and an increasing number of fortifications throughout the Kazakh region.

The defeat in the Crimean War (1854-56) forced the Russian government to refrain from an aggressive policy in relation to Kazakhstan and to adopt economic and political measures to achieve its goals. The process of incorporating Kazakhstan into the Russian Empire, which had been underway for some one hundred and fifty years, was completed around the middle of the nineteenth century.

In comparison with other major European states, Russia was a country with a very reactionary and retarded socio-political structure. National oppression was more severe than in neighbouring states, taking the form of denying almost all rights to the minority peoples, suppression of their culture and forced Russification, and deformation of their economic development to meet the demands of the Russian bourgeoisie and government.

To check the rise of national resistance, the tsarist authorities reinforced the European Cossack settlements in Kazakhstan, which became the base of four Cossack armies. Naturally enough, the increasing colonial oppression aroused deep resentment among the Kazakh masses and popular liberation movements arose on the steppe: the rebellions led by Syrym Datov (1783-97) and by Isatay Taymanov and Makhambet Utemisov (1837-38). In 1837 and 1847, a fierce struggle against tsarist rule was waged by the Kazakhs of the Middle Horde, headed by Kenisary Kasymov, a descendant of the famous Abylay Khan. After seven years of unsuccessful fighting with the rebels, in 1845 the government sent two embassies to Kenisary's headquarters, but he refused to take an oath of allegiance to the Tsar. In a battle with the Kirgiz in 1847, Kenisary Kasimov was taken prisoner and executed, and the Kazakhs' ten-year war for their independence ended in defeat.

Aiming to establish its total supremacy, the imperial government gradually reduced the authority of the khans. Finally, by the 'statute on the Siberian Kirgiz', their power was completely abolished.

In the second half of the nineteenth century the resettlement of the Russian peasantry proceeded on an unprecedented scale. In 1889, at a time of agrarian crisis, the government passed a decree on the resettlement of peasants from Russia in Kazakhstan which resulted in seizure of the lands of the Kazakh population on a massive scale.

As a consequence of the intensive resettlement of Russian and other peasants, it transpired at the end of the 1890s that the northern provinces of Kazakhstan had become overpopulated, creating an acute shortage of farmland. Prime Minister Stolypin's solution was the mass movement of peasants to southern Kazakhstan.

This policy was continued in the early twentieth century, so that before 1917 up to 50 million hectares in Kazakhstan had been appropriated by the tsarist authorities, and Russians and Ukrainians made up more than a third of the population. In the decade 1895-1905, almost 300,000 people were resettled in the steppe province of Kazakhstan; in the 1906-10 period, it was more than 770,000. In all, between 1905 and 1916 the Russian peasant population of the steppe region grew to one and a half million.

This radically changed the national make-up of Kazakhstan. According to the census of 1897, the Russian population in the steppe region was 20 per cent, but in 1917 it was already 42 per cent.

The influx of foreign capital increased as Kazakhstan began to be exploited as a source of raw materials. British and French companies became masters of coal and ore mines in the Kazakh lands.

During the First World War and on the eve of the bourgeois democratic revolution of February 1917, the whole Kazakh steppe was engulfed in a popular uprising of an anti-colonial and anti-feudal character. The causes of the rebellion were manifold: the increasing severity of colonial oppression, the confiscation of lands, heavier taxation, the growth of the wealth of landlords and of feudal exploitation, the stirring up of national discord, the sudden worsening of the Kazakhs' condition as a result of the war, and the policy of Russification.

The national freedom movement of 1916, which swept over all Central Asia and Kazakhstan and was directed against colonial rela-

tions and the war, was one of the manifestations of the revolutionary crisis that was coming to a head in Russia.

Punitive expeditions, aimed at destroying the native population, were sent in 1916 against the rebels in the Torgay province led by Amangeldy Imanov, who became a legendary folk hero. These were carried out by specially prepared troops comprised of Cossacks, peasant settlers and Russians from the towns. The forces of the steppe rebels were no match for the war machine of the huge empire, but the rebellion of Amangeldy Imanov can be seen as the first major national liberation uprising in the dominions of tsarist Russia. Moreover, the revolutionary movement in Kazakhstan in many ways helped the Russian political exiles and the organization of their own proletariat.

The Red Empire

The end of tsarist rule was greeted in Kazakhstan as the beginning of political and national liberation. As a result of the February bourgeois revolution, in March 1917 a provisional government was set up in Kazakhstan. At the first Kazakh Assembly, the Alash Orda Party was formed under the leadership of Alikhan Bukeykhanov, Akhmet Baytursynov, Mirzhakup Dolatov and other eminent members of the Kazakh intelligentsia who refused to accept a Soviet-style government and championed the creation of a Kazakh national bourgeois autonomy. Later on, mass executions were carried out of the founders and members of this party, and even those only slightly connected with it, who were accused of counter-revolutionary activities.

The establishment of Soviet power in Kazakhstan, which met with stubborn resistance, was not a rapid process. The armed struggle of the Kazakhs was a major component of the civil war raging in the Russian Empire. During 1919, most of Kazakhstan was liberated from the White Guard, and the civil war came to an end.

In 1920, the Communists formed a government which on 26 August proclaimed the Autonomous Kirgiz Socialist Soviet Republic (a misnomer because of the Russian confusion of the Kirgiz and Kazakh peoples). This joined the newly created Soviet Union in 1922 and the following year was renamed Kazakh. In 1936, after regularization of frontiers, the country became a full, constituent republic of the USSR. According to the design of the Communist Party and Soviet government, the Kazakh people, like all others in the Soviet Union, were to make a swift transition from feudalism to socialism, leaving out the capitalist stage.

As a result of rapid industrialization in the first decades of Soviet rule, Kazakhstan developed into one of the most important industrial regions of the USSR. Coal mining and the oil industry were given high priority, and the mineral wealth of the Kazakh lands was intensively exploited. Metallurgy was developed, as were heavy engineering and the chemical, textile and food processing industries, but in the main the forced industrial growth focused on the production of raw materials.

Soviet agricultural policy imposed collectivization of farms and forced the nomadic-herding population to settle, thereby destroying the traditional economy and way of life of the Kazakh peasantry. This resulted in terrible famine and genocide. In the famine from 1931 to 1933, the number of Kazakhs alone who died of starvation is estimated at between one and a half and three million. Close on a million Kazakhs emigrated to China, Iran, Afghanistan and elsewhere.

Stalin's policy of collectivization and the Soviet system of coercion with its profoundly inhuman ideology caused a tragedy far greater in scale than any other in the history of the Kazakh people.

The formation of collective farms was accompanied by a struggle with the wealthier members of society: the beys (rich land and cattle owners) and *kulaks* (well-to-do farmers). In 1930 and 1931, 6,765 peasants were exiled from Kazakhstan and, at the same time, 46,091 *kulak* families from Russia and other republics were deported to Kazakhstan. These policies provoked intense hostility and some four hundred popular uprisings, which were put down in the most cruel manner. The records for 1938 show over 1,317,000 people in concentration camps, 355,000 in penal colonies, and 350,000 in prisons.

As part of the Soviet Union, Kazakhstan, took part in the Great Patriotic War (1941-45), as the Second World War was called in the USSR. The whole economy of the country was geared to the war effort, working at full capacity to supply the front with everything necessary. Hundreds of factories were moved here from the western regions of the USSR, and Kazakhstan received tens of thousands of evacuees from Russia, Ukraine, Belorussia and the Baltic republics.

Among the important projects developed on the territory of Kazakhstan in the post-war years, special mention should be made of the Semipalatinsk nuclear testing ground and the Baykonur cosmodrome in Kyzyl-Orda province, which was the main cosmodrome of the Soviet space programme. The world's first cosmonaut, Yuri Gagarin, was launched into space at Baykonur. At the Semipalatinsk testing ground, nuclear devices equal to 2,500 Hiroshima bombs were exploded from 1949 to 1968. The most powerful bomb of 150 megatons was tested there.

The Collapse of the Soviet Union. The campaign in the 1950s under the slogan: 'All for the opening up of the virgin lands' provided further proof of the unreliability of the centralized planning system administered by bureaucrats. The scheme of ploughing up vast areas of Kazakhstan for grain production was poorly planned and took too little account of the climatic and soil conditions. As a result, after a few good harvests, yields drastically declined and there was widespread soil erosion.

The period of economic, political and social stagnation in all the republics of the USSR that began in the 1970s had brought the country to a state of serious crisis by the middle of the 1980s. The programme of *perestroika* (restructuring), which was then introduced, was welcomed by Kazakhstan and the other republics as a harbinger of political and economic change, but the failure to carry it through finally confirmed the impossibility of re-animating the Soviet empire in the existing political framework.

The obvious contradiction between the actual dictates from Moscow and the declared democracy of *perestroika* was a source of dissatisfaction and unrest among young Kazakhs. On 17-18 December 1986 this led to tragic consequences and loss of lives in the main square of Almaty.

In 1989 Nursultan Nazarbaev, an active supporter of reforms, took up the leadership of Kazakhstan, and two years later was elected President of the Republic by a national referendum.

On 16 December 1991, the country officially declared its independence and began a new page in its history as the Republic of Kazakhstan.

CULTURE

The establishment of feudal relations in Kazakhstan, which was continually at war, and the movement from the east of large tribal unions, some of whom settled in the region, influenced both the economic and political history of the country and the development of culture and learning. It was also significant that only limited sections of society, connected with the feudal nobility, took part in the cultural, historical process. Internal and external troubles often led to the destruction of the earlier scholarly and artistic achievements. Some states and peoples disappeared, as during the Mongol invasion, when towns became ruins, links with the outside world were broken, and culture, crafts, trade and other economic activity fell into decline. After the Mongol invasions, the Kazakhs had to repel the onslaughts of foreign raiders from Jungaria and other neighbouring countries. Moreover, the incessant strife among the feudal nobility was an obstacle to the unification of the people and the steady advancement of art, culture and learning.

From the sixth to the eighth century, an oral poetry tradition was formed among the Turkic tribes, from which original literature later developed. In the period from the ninth to the twelfth century, important literary and scholarly works were created. The *Tarihi-i-Rashidi* of Muhammad Haydar Doglati, the sixteenth-century historian and statesman of Mughulistan and Eastern Turkestan, was the first work to give a full account of the origins of the Kazakhs. The formation of the melodious Kazakh language, and with it the development of a musical culture, coincided with the emergence of a Kazakh national identity.

Representational art on the territory of Kazakhstan dates back to prehistoric rock paintings, stone sculptures and objects of applied art depicting hunting scenes, real and fantastic beasts, and sometimes religious subjects.

Architecture and Towns

The architectural skill of the Saks (Scythians), seen in monuments of the fourth to the second century BC—Jeti-Asar, Chirik-Rabat, the mausoleum of Babish-mullah—displays features that served as the basis of architecture in Central Asia, Kazakhstan and the Near East.

The first towns grew up beside the walls of feudal castles in which the leaders lived, and became centres of trade and craft. The most important cities in the Middle Ages were Ispidjab, Otrar, Taraz, Kulan, Suyab, Merke, Balasagun, Kasribas and Yasy, flourishing cultural and political centres, through which the Silk Road passed up the end of the fifteenth century.

Architecture reached its zenith from the ninth to twelfth centuries, under the Karakhanids. At this time, fired bricks were already being used for building. Dozens of new towns sprang up and the old cities were reinforced and developed. Sygnak, the centre of the Kypchak union, was the main town on the Syr Darya. Otrar, mentioned many times in literary sources, was the most important of all the cities in the region. Excavations there have revealed seven levels, dating from different periods in the town's history, with remains of material culture from the first centuries AD to the first quarter of the eighteenth century.

The Silk Road played a vital role in urban development. The towns of the Jeti Su area traded with Byzantium, Iran, Central Asia, the Caucasus, the Altai, Siberia and Eastern Turkestan. A money economy developed alongside barter trade. The representatives of the ruling

95. The yurt, the traditional mobile home of the nomads, was skilfully constructed to protect against both burning heat and extreme cold, for in the past, herders lived in yurts all year round.

96. The pastures of Kazakhstan are so broad that the herdsman can follow his livestock only on horseback (overleaf).

97. Herders today spend their winters in permanent settlements and live in yurts only in summer, when the herds and flocks are taken to the summer grazing areas. (pp .132-3)

128

102-105. *The Kazakhs love their traditional homes. Nimble hands and age-old skills turn the yurt into a real gallery of applied art. During important festivals in Almaty and other towns, each region exhibits yurts in the city squares. (pp. 138-41)*

*106. The ingenious construction of the
yurt allows it to be taken down or erected
in an hour (overleaf).*

clans minted coins with their own seals. In the thirteenth century, Ispidjab, Otrar and many other towns had mints producing gold, silver and copper dinars.

The writings of Plano Carpini and Wilhelm Rubruk, and the travel notes of the Armenian King Khatum I (from 1253) and the Italian traveller Francesco Pegolotti (from 1340) mention the trade centres of Saraychik, Otrar, Iki-Oguz and Kaylak.

The flourishing of learning and culture in the countries of the Middle and Near East owed much to the devising, back in the ninth and tenth centuries, of special arithmetical and geometrical formulae which could be applied to architecture. These were widely used among medieval builders to calculate the proportions of architectural forms. The mausoleums of Babadji-hatun (tenth to eleventh century), Karahan (eleventh century) and Juban-ata (eleventh to twelfth century), bear witness to the high level of monumental religious architecture in the Karakhanid age. A typical example of the unified type of memorial structure of that time is the mausoleum of Aysha-bibi (eleventh to twelfth century). Its ornamental carvings embody all the motifs of Kazakh folk ornamentation, some of which date back to the times of the Saks.

A unique architectural masterpiece built in the fourteenth and early fifteenth century is the mausoleum-mosque of Hodja Akhmet Yasavi, in the town of Yasy (now called Turkestan), the former capital of Turkestan's rulers and an important religious centre which is still a place of Muslim pilgrimage.

This grandiose mausoleum was raised over the grave of Hodja Akhmet Yasavi by Timur (Tamerlane) and intended at the same time as an enduring testimony of the great conqueror's power. During the period of the Kazakh khanate, it was used as the burial place of khans and other dignitaries, among them Abylay Khan, one of the most outstanding statesmen of Kazakhstan.

The mausoleum was covered on the inside and externally with pale blue and white tiles, and decorated with mosaic and painted majolica. Terracotta tiles were used to face the walls. This magnificent structure has 30 rooms and a central hall surmounted by a dome 18.2 metres in diameter, the biggest in Central Asia and Kazakhstan. A very valuable, large cauldron, cast from an alloy of seven metals, stands within the mausoleum. For almost six centuries this building has never ceased to impress visitors by its imposing size, and to delight them with its matchless beauty: its lavish ornamentation, the gleaming central dome and walls with their glazed tiles, and the decorative cupolas at the corners.

This memorial was highly influential in the development of Kazakh architecture: its individual parts were much imitated in later years and its compositional scheme was repeated in the construction of mosques. A remarkable ensemble of monuments and buildings was later erected around the mausoleum of Hodja Akhmet Yasavi.

In the cemetery of the town of Saraychik, not far from Yasy, there were fine mausoleums of the Kazakh khans Janybek, Kasym, Esim and Jangir, but unfortunately these have not survived.

Unlike the impressive monumental buildings, the houses of the Kazakhs were exceptionally simple and modest, without decoration or luxury: low, unprepossessing structures with flat roofs and domestic outbuildings close by. The unpretentious form of the dwellings was dictated by the conditions of nomadic life and the ever-present neces-

107. The interior decor creates a warm, cosy atmosphere inside the yurt. The living and cooking areas can be separated by curtains or brightly coloured screens woven from rushes.

145

sity of defence against raids from neighbouring peoples.

The yurt (tent), that unsurpassed example of nomadic ingenuity, has survived to the present day from the Sak (Scythian) period. This light, portable dwelling keeps out the cold and winds in winter, and is cool in summer. It is easily erected and taken down, and can be carried on horses or carts. According to its form, purpose and construction, the yurt is divided into three main types: ceremonial for important guests, for dwelling, and for the protection of produce and everyday objects.

The circular framework of the yurt consisted of latticed sections of wooden slats (*kerege*) with curved poles on the upper part, joined at the top to a circle of wood with a crosspiece. The sides were lined with rush matting, and the whole frame had an outer covering of felt. The structural elements are held together by strips of carpeting, woven from different coloured woollen yarn. The doors of richer yurts were decorated with delicate carving, bone incrustation or murals. A felt curtain decorated with appliqué work was rolled up above the doorway and could be let down when necessary. The size of the yurt depended on the number of latticed sections. Rich yurts were covered in white felt. Inside the walls were hung with brightly coloured rugs, and the floor was strewn with strips of felt and carpet. The hearth, on which food was cooked, was in the centre of the yurt. The aperture at the top, which could be covered over at night, served as a source of light and allowed the smoke to escape.

The eminent Kazakh scholar and Enlightener Chokan Valikhanov wrote: 'After a hot, tiring day of hard work, how especially pleasant it is to lie in the yurt on a cool evening, to open the felt panels of the yurt so that the air flows through, and to rest.'

In the eyes of the ancient nomads, the yurt in its structure was a microcosm of the Universe. Today it is regarded as a unique memorial of the material and spiritual culture of the people and an outstanding example of their applied art.

From the fifteenth to the eighteenth century, the types of architectural structure became more varied as a result of the formation of the Kazakh khanates and the inclusion into the state of many new tribes. In the cities, crafts developed: the making of pottery and glass, trades connected with smelting and working metals, the weaving of cloth and rugs, leather working, carving on bone and the fashioning of jewelry. Vessels for everyday use made of stamped earthenware with very interesting moulded elements display a high degree of skill and artistry. The level attained in the art of stone carving can be judged from the richly ornamented doors of the mausoleum of Hodja Akhmet Yasavi. The craft of jewelry making was particularly highly developed, as can be seen from the treasure trove of jewelry and silver ingots found in Otrar.

In the era when Kazakhstan was being incorporated into the Russian Empire, a period of development of industry and the broadening of trade and economic relations with Central Russia, about thirty new towns sprang up and some four hundred Cossack settlements were established. Some of these were settlements housing miners or factory workers and were located near the old towns and in the regions with rich natural resources. Many were military and administrative centres. The former military strongholds in various regions—Uralsk, Aktau, Orenburg, Orsk, Troitsk, Pavlodar, Semipalatinsk, Ust-Kamenogorsk and Verny—gradually became urbanized and grew into new cultural and economic centres.

The vast expanse of the territory of Kazakhstan with a range of climatic conditions, as well as the varied ethnic structure of the population and their different traditions, were factors that influenced the construction of dwellings and other buildings. The interior corresponded to functional needs, while the façades were often in the style of Russian classicism prevalent in the second half of the nineteenth century.

The influence of the Muslim religion was also evident. Some nineteenth-century religious buildings of architectural significance revived the traditions of monumental architecture of earlier periods but with the use of new materials and building techniques.

Fourteen towns in Kazakhstan have more than 100,000 inhabitants: Almaty, Karagandy, Semipalatinsk, Shimkent, Pavlodar, Ust-Kamenogorsk, Jambyl, Akmola, Petropavlovsk, Aktobe, Uralsk, Kostanay, Kyzyl-Orda and Mangystau. All of them are administrative centres of provinces. Many of these cities, together with their nearby settlements, which are almost towns in the own right, are also important centres of industry. There are a dozen medium-sized towns with between 50,000 and 100,000 inhabitants. More than 65 per cent of the towns are small, with a population of under 50,000.

The capital of the republic of Kazakhstan is Almaty (formerly Alma-Ata), a garden city located in the attractive Zaili Alatau foothills, on the northern spurs of the Tien Shan.

The flourishing town of Alma-Ata, through which passed the caravans on the Great Silk Road, was once well known to the Arabs, Chinese and Persians. In the thirteenth century it was completely destroyed during the Mongol invasion, but in time the town of Verny grew up on its ruins. In 1921 its original name was restored. In January 1993, the Supreme Soviet adopted the new Constitution of the Republic of Kazakhstan, in which Almaty was designated the capital of the sovereign state.

The population of Almaty, approaching 1.2 million, includes people of more than a hundred nationalities. In addition to its political and administrative importance, it is a major centre of industrial and scientific activity, with engineering, electric power production and metallurgy, and numerous institutes engaged in research into most areas of modern science. The National Academy of Sciences of the Republic of Kazakhstan unites 43 such institutes.

The capital is also a cultural centre where many writers, poets, artists, composers, musicians and actors live and work. It has 10 theatres, 12 museums, 21 institutions for higher education and 24 semi-specialized education institutes. In the field of the information media and publishing, there are 10 radio and TV channels, 10 publishers and seven printers.

The population is served by 33 hospitals and 126 polyclinics and out-patient clinics. There are 10 research institutes with a staff of 96 doctors and 366 post-graduate students. The institutes of eye diseases, virology and microbiology are well-known abroad for their research.

In the attractive environs of Almaty an extensive 'health zone' has been created with sanatoria, rest homes, camps for schoolchildren and tourist camps.

As the hub of external trade and cultural relations, the city promotes contacts between Kazakh institutions, enterprises and banks, and representatives of foreign firms, foreign investors and embassies.

Literature

Literature, the most important part of the cultural heritage of the Kazakh people, expressed their world-view, their ideals, self-awareness and their moral and aesthetic values.

Throughout the ages, the steppe dwellers had a high appreciation of the skilful use of language, and possessed an exceptional talent for oratory, story-telling and poetry.

Adolf Jan Janushkevich, the Polish scholar, who was present at a session of Kazakh *biis* (judges), wrote: 'A few days ago I witnessed a confrontation between two contesting parties and, to my surprise, found myself applauding the orators, who had never even heard of Demosthenes and Cicero. Today the poets had a competition. They do not know how to read or write, but their talent amazed me. A people on whom the Creator has bestowed such abilities cannot remain alien to civilization; its spirit will some day penetrate into the Kazakh deserts, will fan the little sparks, and there will come a time when the now nomadic population will take an honoured place among the peoples who look down on them, as the higher castes of India look down on the unfortunate pariahs.'

Kazakh oral literature, rooted in the ancient past, includes many genres: legends, fables, proverbs and sayings, ritual songs, heroic and lyric epics...

The old Turkic runic writings, found among all Turkic peoples, record early examples of the Kazakh oral poetry tradition. In the sixth and seventh centuries the Turkic-speaking tribes of Central Asia which came under the Turkic khanate, and also the western Turkic tribes of the Lower Volga, the Don and the North Caucasus which created the Khazar state, were already using their own script.

Written sources tell us that the Turki carved symbols on small wooden boards for counting 'the requested amounts of people, horses, taxes, and livestock'. The Turkic ambassador, the Sogdian Manakh, who was in Constantinople at the court of Justinian, brought with him a missive from the Turkic kagan, written in 'Sak script'.

One of the oldest inscriptions, a record of the events of the first thirty years of the existence of the Turkic kaganate, carved on the Burgut stele on the burial mound of Kagan Taspar (572-81), indicates that the Sogdian script was understood by quite a broad circle of educated people in the kaganate.

Around the same time, the Buddhist work *Nirvana Sutra*, which was to exert considerable influence among the Turki, was first translated into Turkic using the Sogdian script. Later this script was called 'Uygur', since the Uygurs used it from the ninth to the fifteenth century.

In the second half of the seventh century, on the basis of the Sogdian writing, with a few additional symbols, the first Turkic script was created. This ancient Turkic writing was first discovered in the Yenisey valley in the 1720s by D. Messerschmidt, a German scholar in the service of Tsar Peter I, who was accompanied by a captured Swedish officer, I. Stralenberg. Because of its similarity with Scandinavian runic texts, they called the writing 'runic'.

In 1889 the Russian scholar N. M. Yadrintsev discovered huge stone stelae with runic inscriptions in the valley of the River Orkhon in northern Mongolia. The Danish scholar, V. Thomsen, who found the key to the script, and the Russian Turkic scholar V. V. Radlov deciphered the inscriptions and provided the first coherent reading of them. This writing was given the name Orkhono-Yenisey, after the place where these monuments were found. Other monuments with runic writing have been discovered in northern Mongolia, on the territory of Tuva and Khakasia, in the Baikal region, the Altai, Eastern Turkestan, and elsewhere in Central Asia and Kazakhstan.

Lengthy runic texts found on the territory of the Turkic kaganate, Mongolia and the Yenisey region are both important historical documents and literary works. The most famous runic inscriptions are in honour of Kagan Bilge and his brother Kul-tegin (dating from 732 to 735), and also the adviser to the early rulers, Tonykok (716).

In the Karakhanid epoch the formation of the literary language of the Turkic-speaking peoples on the broad territory of Central Asia and present-day Kazakhstan was completed.

After the acceptance of Islam in Kazakhstan, Arabic literature became widespread. The contemporary scholar and encyclopedist Abu Nasr al-Farabi, who had received his education in Kypchak, one of the dialects of ancient Turkic, wrote treatises in Arabic and old Turkic on orthography, calligraphy, versification, rhetoric, as well as great philosophical quatrains. His famous *Treatise on Music* has been translated into many foreign languages. In his mathematical works, he devised arithmetical and geometrical calculations which formed the basis of construction and the architecture of the Near and Middle East. Besides al-Farabi, a whole galaxy of important poets, writers and scholar-historians came from the Turkic-Kypchak milieu.

Makhmud Kashgari's *Divan Lugat at-Turki* is a brilliant testimony to the cultural level of the Turkic peoples in the eleventh century. The wide-ranging contents of this work, a real encyclopedia of Turkic life in the early Middle Ages, allow one to judge the high level of philosophy and scholarship of that time. It is of special significance for the study of the ethnic history and geography of the Turkic lands.

Yusuf Galasaguni, one of the highly educated Turkic poets and writers of the eleventh century, is best known for his original treatise, *Kutadgu Bilik*, a profound didactic, philosophical work in the ancient Turkic language. It was written in 1069 and presented as a gift to

Bogra, a ruler of the Karakhanid dynasty. The works of Ahmet Yugnaki, who continued the didactic tradition of Turkic literature begun by Galasaguni, have a special place in the history of the Turkic-speaking peoples.

The *Korkut ata Kitabi* ('The Book of My Grandfather Korkut') is one of the most original literary works of medieval Oguz-Kypchak literature. It conveys the patriotic feelings of the Oguz and Kypchaks who fought for their homeland.

The *Divan* (compilation of writings) of Hodja Ahmet Yasavi was written, unusually for that time, in the Kypchak Oguz dialect of ancient Turkic. Ahmet Yasavi, a Sufi poet and famous Muslim teacher, is revered as the second saint after Muhammad. He is buried in a mosque in the city of Turkestan, known as Little Mecca.

One of the most valuable Turkic literary works of the Middle Ages is the *Oguzname*, based on legends current during the rule of the Oguz. One of the early variants of the *Oguzname* is preserved in copies made by Rashid Addin in the thirteenth century, but a later and more complete version was left in manuscript by the eighteenth-century historian Abulgazy. The eminent Kazakh scholar of the nineteenth century Chokan Valikhanov, as well as P. Pellyu and V. Bartold, gave a final version of the *Oguzname* to the Kazakhs.

The oral folk tradition was, of course, an important factor in the development of written literature. It not only provided a stimulus for its appearance, but has remained an inexhaustible source of inspiration.

Poetry flourished in Kazakh literature from the fifteenth to the eighteenth century. It reflected the historical events of the period of the formation of the Kazakh khanate and the Kazakh national identity. A leading role was played by the *jyrau*, who were poets who could improvise verse for any occasion, story-tellers, soothsayers and prophets. They praised the chivalrous ideals of the medieval warrior-nomad, his morality and world-view, and were experts in the retelling of legends, customs and the genealogy of tribes and peoples.

In the period of cruel wars, the *jyrau* took part in many campaigns, accompanying the soldiers into battle and inspiring them with their verses. Some themselves became heroic knights and commanders. They created poems on many themes connected with military life. The *jyrau* was not only a literary figure, but also, more often than not, a mentor of the khans and sultans and took an active part in the political life of society. Many of them left behind a vast heritage of poems.

The nineteenth century marked a new stage in the history of Kazakh literature. Makhambet Utemisov (1804-46) was known as a fiery poet, a brave warrior who used the word and the sword to fight for the soul and the survival of his people. A warrior-poet of rebellious character, uncompromising in the struggle against the might of the khans and tsars, he was the leader of the Bukeev Orda rebellion. He fell at the hand of a hired assassin. His poems express the power of his personality and love of freedom. Makhambet's original poetry enriched Kazakh literature with both ideas and themes.

A literature developed in the Kazakh language based on the fine oral tradition, but Kazakh was raised to the level of an international literary language only in the nineteenth century, thanks to the poetic art of Abai (Ibrahim) Kunanbaev (1845-1904).

A great thinker, man-of-letters, composer and tireless Enlightener, Abai was the genius of his time, an outstanding personality of Kazakhstan. By the age of thirteen, he had mastered the Arabic,

Persian, Chagatay and Russian languages, which allowed him in the following years to gain a deep knowledge of the classics of the East. He also had a lively interest in classical literature and the philosophical thought of Europe and Russia, whose works had a beneficial effect on his formation as a matchless master of the artistic word. He made brilliant translations into Kazakh of works by Pushkin, Lermontov, Krylov, Goethe, Schiller and Byron.

Abai created immortal works not only in poetry, but also in music. His prose, *The Book of Words*, is a religio-philosophic treatise, expressing all the profundity of the people's wisdom, and imbued with love of all humanity and the Creator of all living things. Abai is the national pride of the Kazakh people. In 1995 UNESCO is marking the 150th anniversary of the great Kazakh poet.

The beginning of the twentieth century brought an irreplaceable loss to the culture, literature and learning of Kazakhstan. A whole galaxy of outstanding poets, writers and scholars, the finest representatives of the intelligentsia, who were the light and hope of Kazakhstan, were falsely accused of nationalistic views hostile to the socialist order and annihilated by the Stalinist regime. These were the founders of Kazakh literature of the Soviet period: S. Seyfullin, A. Baytursynov, M. Dulatov, I. Jansugurov, J. Aymauytov, S. Kudajberdyev and hundreds of other gifted persons engaged in the fields of literature, the arts and scholarship.

Mukhtar Auezov, an outstanding writer, scholar and dramatist of the Soviet period, played a significant role in the establishment of realistic prose on a high professional level. He was the author of many short stories, novellas, plays and an epic novel, *The Way of Abai*, which has been translated into many languages.

The Arts

Figurative and Applied Art. The original and exceptionally interesting culture of the nomadic peoples of this region was recorded in artistic media in the most important stages of its centuries-long development. The rock-face depictions of animals from Palaeolithic and Neolithic times, and the stone totem carvings of animals, cave and rock-face paintings of hunting scenes and pottery vessels with geometric designs that survive from the Bronze Age, demonstrate the antiquity and high level of the artistic production in early nomadic society. The famous Sak-Siberian 'wild beast' style of art of the Saks (also called Scythians) is exemplified by the bronze and silver artefacts discovered in the Issyk burial mound, a treasure trove of world cultural significance.

In the Middle Ages cult and memorial structures proliferated on the territory of Kazakhstan. Tombstones and sarcophagi, richly decorated with carving, mosaic and sculptures of animals, show that from olden times Kazakh craftsmen attained a high level of skill and artistry in the plastic arts. The development of cult or religious figurative art and sculpture ceased with the acceptance of Islam by the nomads.

The traditions of folk art have undoubtedly exerted an influence on contemporary fine art, which began to develop after the October Revolution. Russian artists from Moscow and Leningrad made a significant contribution to the training and notable achievements of twentieth-century Kazakh artists. During the seven decades of Soviet power, several generations of painters and sculptors created original

108-110. Hunting with birds of prey was one of the most popular forms of recreation among the Kazakhs of old. The 'kusbegi', the name given to expert hunters and connoisseurs of this sport, were highly esteemed in their community (pp. 153-7).

works which form part of the artistic heritage of Kazakhstan.

Over the centuries the applied arts reached a very high level of skill and sophistication, particularly in the fashioning of jewelry. Craftsmen also engaged in the decoration of weapons and armour, horse's accoutrements, hunting equipment and traditional musical instruments. The interior of the yurt was embellished with finely woven textiles and rugs, and carved and engraved objects of wood, bone and metal. The production of felt, carpets and rushwork was inherited by the Kazakhs from their Turki and Kypchak ancestors. The artefacts of applied art and the ornamentation of Kazakh architecture are generally distinguished by a bright decorativeness, a subtle grasp of colour and form, and brilliant mastery of execution.

Music. The Kazakh national *melos*, the musical culture of the bardic tradition, began to be formed when the Kazakh national identity took shape. Eye witnesses—Marco Polo, Wilhelm Rubruk, Ruzbekhan, Takub, Plano Carpini—speak of the importance of music in the life of the nomads.

The songs and instrumental music of the Kazakh people embodied their history over the centuries, their struggle for justice, hopes and expectations; their music was a reflection of their soul, of their cultural and moral level.

Many of the composers of the past were well-educated for their time. All of them were literate, and some knew the Arabic, Persian and Russian languages, but they could not read or write music. Their works formed part of the vast ocean of anonymous folk music, the accumulated riches of the past centuries preserved in the oral tradition. Popular music achieved its peak in pre-revolutionary Kazakhstan, in the work of the galaxy of professional composer-performers of the nineteenth century: Kurmangazy Sagyrbaev, Tattimbet Kazangapov, Ikhlasa Dukenov, Abai Kunanbaev, Shakarim Kudayberdyev.

In medieval times there were some two dozen types of musical instrument, but many fell out of use because they had a limited range of notes or were of similar timbre. Thanks to the tireless research of music scholars, these have now been restored and refined.

Kazakh music in the Soviet period drew on the finest achievements of folk music and on Russian and Western European classics. The fundamental aspects of the national music have been preserved and developed in modern forms by composers and performers.

Ballet. When the Kazakh ballet was formed, the authentic forms of folk dances had long been lost, though their existence among the Kazakhs is confirmed by the presence in the national language of the word 'dance' (*bi*) and 'to dance' (*bileu*). The complex process of developing Kazakh choreography went hand in hand with the recreation of folk dances. Choreography, as an independent art form, appeared in the republic at the beginning of the 1930s. The distinguished ballet master A. Alexandrov, who came to Kazakhstan from Moscow, played a major role in the development of the ballet company, which was established in 1933. In the war years, Kazakh artists were able to benefit by working with leading ballet artists of the Soviet Union who were evacuated to Kazakhstan. The company's repertoire was extended by the addition of classic works such as 'Giselle' and 'Swan Lake'. In particular, the eminent ballerina Galina Ulanova left her mark on the development of the national ballet.

Theatre. The origins of the Kazakh theatre are to be found in ceremonials, games, and the performances of comic actors, wits, clowns

162

and other popular entertainers.

After the October Revolution, many drama groups and theatrical companies were organized, and conditions were created for the development of the dramatic arts and a national theatre. This was inextricably bound up with the many-faceted work and dramatic talent of Mukhtar Auezov, who started his career as a playwright. The Kazakh State Musical Theatre, now called the Abai State Academic Theatre of Opera and Ballet, was founded in 1934.

The Kazakh theatre today is notable for its variety of trends, forms and genres. It continues to explore the artistic traditions of the people, adopts a creative approach to the classical heritage and draws on modern theatrical achievements. In multinational Kazakhstan, as well as the Kazakh, there are Russian, Uygur, Korean and German theatres.

The works of western playwrights—Shakespeare, Molière, Schiller and others—have been well translated. Their performances in these classics are high points in the careers of outstanding Kazakh actors such as K. Kuanishbaev and Shaken Aymanov. In the 1960s the talented director A. Membetov entered the theatrical life of the republic. As a prominent Kazakh director he opened up a new world of Kazakh attitudes, staging performances that brought out the philosophic content of the plays.

Film. No films were made in pre-revolutionary Kazakhstan, and very few in the inter-war period. The first documentaries were shot in the mid 1920s. The development of Kazakh literature and art, and the experience gained in documentary films bore fruit in 1938 in the film 'Amangeldy', which marked the birth of the art of cinematography in Kazakhstan. The documentary film-makers became especially active in the years of the Great Patriotic War, when all artists were called upon to play their part in rallying the people to defeat the enemy. The wartime film production in the Almaty studios by Russian and Ukrainian masters of cinematography greatly benefited the artistic development of Kazakh film-makers. The dozens of films of various genres which they have produced in recent years include feature films awarded prizes at international film festivals. The outstanding theatre and cinema director Shaken Aymanov is still regarded as the supreme Kazakh film-maker.

The Circus. The art of the circus, so beloved by the Kazakhs, is closely related to their former nomadic way of life. Its early forms appeared in various games, in deft, elegant movements while galloping on horseback, communicating ideas by mime and making onlookers laugh with gestures and movements. Horses were trained not only for riding and pulling or carrying loads, but also for the performance of various manoeuvres and tricks at speed. Mastery of the use of the bow and arrow, spear, sabre and mace while at full gallop, and catching the right moment to enter into single combat with an opponent, were practised daily and served as compulsory military training for the warriors of that time.

The first steps in circus art were taken with such tricks as bending over the mane of the horse and the saddle-bow, riding on the side of the horse or under its belly, hooked on to the saddle girth, picking up a fallen weapon off the ground, and many other national games. These difficult exercises carried out on a galloping horse were gradually perfected and formed the basis of such national games as mock-combat involving several people trying to drag each other out of the saddle, picking up coins and rings off the ground, and *kokpar*, a game somewhat like polo but played with a dead goat as 'ball'. Many elements of the equestrian performances in the circus have their origin in these games.

The Kazakh people always had a high appreciation of strength, skill, agility and beauty of movement, and took delight in watching wrestlers, men of the people who were endowed with giant strength and demonstrated incredible moves. Stories and legends about them were passed on by word of mouth, and songs and long poems were dedicated to them. Prior to the October Revolution, the famous Kazakh wrestler Hadjimukan gave amazing demonstrations of his skill and strength in circus arenas, which brought him enormous popularity.

The forerunners of the circus artists were various performers who entertained the public with their feats and tricks: wrestlers would lie under boards over which a camel was made to walk, or would display their muscular control by performing rhythmical movements. There were tumblers who rolled over and over in the middle of a big wheel, stilt walkers and others who did various tricks to amuse and surprise the spectators.

The organization in 1965 of the Almaty studio of circus art did much to improve the level and variety of such shows in Kazakhstan, which has an excellent permanent circus company.

Science and Scholarship

The origins of scientific thought in Kazakhstan date back to the distant past. The conquest of Central Asia and Kazakhstan by the Arabs brought Islam to the region, but the local cultures and languages did not disappear, though Arabic, like Latin in Europe, became the lingua franca on the territory of the caliphate. Arab culture became a synthesis of the cultures of many peoples, including those of Central Asia and Kazakhstan. An exceptionally active role in its development was played by gifted persons from the countries conquered by the Arabs.

The medieval towns of Kazakhstan were famous not only for their bazaars and trades, but also for their poets, scholars and artists, their rich libraries and educational institutions. The main centres of science, culture and art were the towns of Otrar, Taraz, Valasagun, Sygnak and Sauran. The most important of these was Otrar (Farab), the old capital of the Turkic peoples, lying on the Silk Road from India and China to Europe, which crossed the settled farming and nomadic herding regions of Central Asia and Kazakhstan. In its wealth of manuscripts and books, the Otrar library was second only to the Alexandria library in Egypt. The prominent philosopher, scholar and encyclopedist Abu Nasr al-Farabi, who was born in Otrar, left behind a vast heritage: almost a hundred works on astronomy, astrology, mathematics, philosophy, logic, medicine, natural history, sociology, linguistics, ethics, rhetoric, music and poetry. Among the inhabitants of Otrar, Buruni, ibn-Siny (Avicenna), Nasr at-Din at-Tusi and Rudaki all played a significant role in the development of culture and the dissemination of knowledge. Other distinguished figures were the astronomer and mathematician Gabbas Jaukhari (first half of the ninth century), who collaborated with Khorezmi in devising astronomic tables, and his contemporaries Iskhak al-Farabi and Ismail Jaukhari, compilers of a dictionary of some forty thousand words. The noted geographer and historian Janakh ibn-Khakan al-Kimaki emerged from the Kymak tribe in the Irtysh region.

The achievements of the scholars and artists of the East was recognized even then, as can be seen from the fact that from the tenth to the twelfth century the works of these scholars, scientists and poets were translated and circulated in France, Italy, Spain and other European countries.

The *Canon of Medicine* by ibn-Siny, *Algebra and Exercises* by al-Khorezmi and the ideas of al-Farabi were disseminated indirectly through the works of ibn-Rushdie (1126-98), Giordano Bruno (1548-1600) and Baruch (Benedictus) de Spinoza (1632-77).

Discussing the advances of learning in Central Asia and Kazakhstan in the ninth and tenth centuries, the orientalist N. I. Conrad (1891-1970) introduced the term 'the Eastern renaissance', underlining the scope and creativity of the cultural and scientific achievements of that age.

Knowledge derived from and connected with their way of life was accumulated by the tribes and peoples inhabiting the territory of Kazakhstan. At the basis of the calculation of the calendar lay the knowledge of the stars and their different constellations by which they could set their course when on the move. The cosmogonical ideas of the Kazakhs were attuned to the life they led and the spiritual needs of the society. The constellation of the Great Bear was called *Jeti Karaktsy* or the Seven Robbers, the Pole Star was *Temir Kazyk* ('the Iron Pole'), the Milky Way—*Kus Joly* ('the Birds' Way'). The planet Venus was known as *Sholdan*, Mars was *Kyzyl Jildiz*, the constellation of the Pleiades was *Urker*, and so on.

At the end of the seventeenth century and beginning of the eighteenth, the territory and population of Kazakhstan, its history, culture and everyday life and traditions, became the subject of research by scholars in Russia and several countries of Western Europe. After Kazakhstan became part of the Russian Empire, scholarly interest increased. Many notes and articles were written about it by the Russian gentry, but only a few could be qualified as serious scientific researchers. One of these was P. I. Rychkov, an official of the chancery of Orenburg province, who wrote *The Topography of the Orenburg Province*. In the eighteenth century two academic expeditions were organized, which left their mark on the study of Kazakhstan. Such studies were carried out both by institutes of learning and by government bodies in pursuit of their expansionist aims.

171

Chokan Valikhanov (1835-65), the pre-eminent Kazakh scholar and leader of the democratic Enlightenment movement, was a key figure of Kazakh national culture. Born into the sultan Chingis family, he received an eastern and western education. While enrolled in the Omsk cadet school, he was taught by such highly educated men as Gonsevsky, Zhdan-Pushkin and Lobanovsky. After graduating, he served as an adjutant to the general governor of Western Siberia. In Omsk, Valikhanov made friends with G. N. Potanin, the exiled writer F. M. Dostoyevsky and the scholar and traveller P. P. Semyonov-Tien Shan. His contacts with the people of the Kazakh steppe—the judges, the sultans, the elders—and with figures of Russian science and literature were spiritually enriching and expanded the breadth of his learning. At that time, Eastern Turkestan was little known, since it was carefully guarded by the Qing dynasty from any contacts with the outside world. Attempts by European scholars and explorers to penetrate it sometimes ended tragically. For instance, in 1857 the German traveller and researcher Adolph Schlagintweit died in Kashgar. The first information on the circumstances of his death was obtained by Chokan Valikhanov. Risking his life, in September 1858 he entered Kashgaria as part of a trade caravan. On the basis of the material he gathered, he subsequently wrote a very scholarly description of the region that was of immense value for Russian and world studies of Central Asia. In the early 1860s, the noted French publicist, Emile Jeuneveau, wrote: 'Thanks to the work of the Russian officer Velikhanov, we now have valuable historical data for the clarification of the political position of Chinese Tartaria.'

Chokan Valikhanov studied the languages, folklore and oral poetry of the peoples of the East, and left some fundamental works on the geography, history and ethnography of the peoples of Central Asia and Kazakhstan. In his short life, Valikhanov succeeded in making a remarkable contribution to world science. His achievements were very highly regarded by Russian scholars, such as the orientalist N. N. Veselovsky, who wrote: 'Chokan Chingisovich Valikhanov flashed like a meteor over the field of eastern scholarship. Russian orientalists unanimously recognized him as a phenomenon and were expecting from him great and important revelations about the destiny of the Turkic peoples, but his premature death deprived us of those expectations.'

Ibray (Ibrahim) Altynsarin (1841-89) was well-known as an outstanding teacher, scholar and public figure. His circle of interests and research was wide—he wrote works on pedagogy, ethnography and folklore. He founded institutions for primary and vocational education of a type previously unknown in Kazakhstan, and devised a Kazakh alphabet on the basis of Russian Cyrillic script. His original school system for the Kazakh population was based on the principle of preserving the national identity. Despite the fact that the tsarist government was not interested in the enlightenment of the Kazakh people and in every way hindered the increase in the number of schools, Altynsarin succeeded in opening primary schools in various provinces of Kazakhstan. With his poetic gifts and his works on pedagogy, history, ethnography and linguistics, Ibray Altynsarin, a scholar and innovator, developed the best national traditions of the Kazakh people, and was instrumental in the formation in Kazakhstan of a scientific world-view on important problems in various fields.

After the October Revolution, scientific activity was reorganized on new principles and primarily directed towards the solving of scientific and technical problems of importance to the state. Expeditions were organized to study the natural resources of Kazakhstan, and in a very short time research institutes were set up. In 1926 a programme of scientific research was drawn up covering the fields of livestock breeding, statistics, the economy, anthropology, ethnography, medicine, soil science, botany, geology and hydro-geology.

In 1932 the Kazakhstan branch of the Academy of Sciences of the USSR was established, followed in 1946 by the Academy of Sciences of Kazakhstan. Its first president was the academician K. Stapaev, the founder of the republic's geological school. The Academy of Sciences of Kazakhstan unites 43 scientific institutes engaged on research into almost all branches of modern science. The most important areas of research are closely bound up with the republic's economic strengths. They include the processes that occur with geological changes in the earth's crust, mining and the effective utilization of mineral resources, and increasing agricultural productivity. Notable research is also being carried out in the fields of social sciences, the economy, history, literature and art, language, philosophy and law.

Religion

In the early Middle Ages the Turkic-speaking population of Kazakhstan was pagan, worshipping the sky and earth-water. The khans believed that they ruled by the will of the sky. The deity next in importance was Umay, the protectress of children and the family hearth. The cult of sacred mountains was also very widespread. The Turki worshipped fire and widely practised the custom of purification by it. Excavations of the citadel of the town of Baba-Ata have shown that one of the halls of the palace complex was used for rites connected with the cult of fire. Evil spirits and diseases were driven out by fire, and those wanting to get rid of their sins passed between two fires. Fire was present, too, in the rites of marriage. The cult of fire co-existed for a time with Islam. According to ancient beliefs, no one should walk across fire, set foot on the hearth or extinguish fire with water. In early, pre-Islamic times, cremation of the dead was practised.

Along with their own beliefs, among the population of Kazakhstan in the ninth to eleventh centuries Buddhism, Manichaeism and Christianity were practised. Buddhism gained favour among the ruling circles of the first Turkic kaganate, and Manichaean and Christian communities existed in many towns.

In the eleventh and twelfth centuries, with the adoption of Islam by a large proportion of the population, pagan cults gradually died out. The first attempts to spread Islam among the Turkic nomads were recorded as early as the eighth century. The fall of the Western Turkic kaganate early in that century speeded up the penetration of Arab conquerors who brought Islam into Central Asia and Kazakhstan, but because of the fragmentation of the tribes the faith did not put down firm roots until the tenth century. It was accelerated by the foundation of the Karluk and other early feudal states on the territory of Kazakhstan whose rulers accepted Islam.

Islam spread further under the Karakhanids (tenth to twelfth centuries), and was adopted by the upper echelons of the Golden Horde in the time of Khan Berk (1255-66). The faith penetrated into the Kazakhstan steppe from Central Asia through missionaries who had come in with trading caravans. An important part in the Islamization of the Kazakhs was played by the Kokand khanate, which was to become a major force in the region in the eighteenth and early nineteenth century.

From the tenth to the thirteenth century many mosques were built in the towns of Kazakhstan, and Kazakhs were among the pilgrims to Mecca and Medina. When the Muslim faith became established as the predominant religion, a whole series of notable scholars devoted themselves to the study of the medieval learning which Islam had brought with it: Arabic language and literature, philosophy and logic. They include Abu Nasr al-Farabi, Iskhak al-Otrari, Jamal al-Turkestani and Kadyrgali Jadari.

At the same time the Islamic mystical movement of Sufism was spreading in Central Asia and Kazakhstan. The sheikhs specially sent out their disciples to the boundaries of the Muslim world with the aim of converting unbelievers to Islam and spreading the faith among the nomads of Kazakhstan. One of the best-known missionaries was Hodja Ahmet Yasavi, who founded his Yasavia order. Later, another order of the Sufis, the Nakshbandia, expanded its influence.

After Kazakhstan became united with Russia, the tsars attempted to spread Christianity among the Kazakhs, but with little success. Recognizing the futility of these efforts, the government changed tack and openly supported Islam, facilitating its spread and strengthening its position. Decrees were issued on the building of mosques and the provision of mullahs for them, and a system of muftis (Muslim spiritual leaders) was organized.

After the printing of books in eastern typography was transferred from St Petersburg to Kazan, this city became one of the centres for spreading Islam.

The Russian settlers in Kazakhstan brought with them the Orthodox Christian faith. There were also members of other Christian churches and sects, which belonged to three main groups: the old Russian sectarianism (Old Believers, Khlysts, Molochans, Dukhobors), churches of western Protestant origin (Baptists, Evangelicals, Seventh Day Adventists) and sects that appeared in Russia in the twentieth century (Jehovah's Witnesses, Pentecostalists and Adventist Reformists).

With the victory of the October Revolution, religion was deprived of its economic basis and under the changed social conditions its influence sharply declined. The Constitution of the Republic of Kazakhstan guarantees freedom of worship and religious belief. At present there are almost 700 mosques, churches and other places of worship in the republic, the majority located in the southern and northern provinces.

The followers of the Sunni branch of Islam have several dozen religious associations, whose leadership provides spiritual guidance to Kazakhstan's Muslims.

Judaism, the Hare Krishna movement and Bahaism also have adherents in the republic.

Pastoral Life

The Kazakh auls ('villages' or migratory communities) were traditionally located on sites that offered favourable conditions for herding or were by tribal association near towns or rural settlements whose inhabitants engaged not only in trade and crafts, but also in livestock and irrigated arable farming. Each aul had a definite number of yurts (tents), its own lands, watering holes and haymaking land.

The nomadic way of life was dictated by the necessity of regularly moving flocks and herds to fresh pastures. Since their well-being depended on both climatic conditions and the quality of pasturage, transhumance was practised.

The nomads passed the winter in so-called wintering areas in the steppe regions, which were often hundreds of kilometres apart. They chose sites protected from winds and blizzards, near hills or in the hollows of meadows with plentiful grass, where there was sufficient grazing for the huge herds of livestock and horses. They lived in covered wagons or yurts, in which they tried to keep the fire constantly burning in the hearth. Compressed dried dung, brushwood and firewood served as fuel.

The summer pastures were mainly in the mountainous regions, where there was higher precipitation and the pasturage was richer. Often they were a great distance from the wintering area, sometimes up to five hundred kilometres away. In this season the nomads lived a more united life than in winter. Despite the distances and difficulties involved, moving camp to the summer pastures was a joyful event. The camels and horses that formed the caravan were decorated with bright rugs, many pendants and little bells. The caravan was usually led by a girl riding on a horse or a camel, accompanied by horsemen and horsewomen dressed in their finery.

Accounts of travellers provide vivid descriptions of how the steppe people moved camp, carrying with them whole houses. The dwellings made of wood and covered with felt were transported on two-wheeled or four-wheeled carts. These were also used to live in and, when placed in a circle around the camp, for defence. Depending on the weight of the load, the carts were drawn by horses, oxen or camels.

According to medieval travellers, the covered carts of the inhabitants of Desht-i-Kypchak were 'movable houses' and, in the words of one writer, they were 'so striking that one is amazed at their beauty, craftsmanship and elegance'. They also describe them as 'castles raised on high', or 'houses built of wood in the air'. At the beginning of the seventeenth century, the cart-houses disappeared from the everyday life of the nomads, replaced by more easily transportable dwellings: the yurts.

Not just auls moved camp, but whole nomadic settlements—a great mass of people and innumerable sheep, cattle, horses and camels in motion across the steppe. The auls that were in the vanguard in moving camp took care not to destroy the grass and bushes, which were vital for those who followed. They kept a sharp eye on the watering holes, the springs and the wells.

The Kazakhs mainly reared four types of livestock: horses, camels, cattle and sheep. These animals were regarded as symbolizing not only material prosperity, but also the four quarters of the world, the four elements, the four characters of man and the four directions.

The horse, considered to be the most sacred and noble animal, figures in proverbs and is eulogized in songs and tales of chivalry. Horse-breeding was highly developed, and almost fifty different colours of coat were recognized. For the Kazakh, the horse is much more than a faithful friend and helper; it is a symbol of the world of ancestral wisdom, of intellect, beauty and nobility. The horse is the spark of God. This relationship is especially expressed in the rites of birth, marriage and burial. A horse is presented as a gift to an esteemed guest, and no festival can go by without equestrian contests.

The steppe horses are endowed with great stamina. In the northern part of Kazakhstan the breeds are stronger and hardier than those in the southern part. Horses are divided according to their use into pack and draft animals, riding and race horses. The renowned Karabair horses raised in some provinces are a mixture of the Turkmen type with local, Bashkir, Mongol, Kalmyk or Don breeds.

The drink made from mare's milk, *koumiss*, is highly prized not only for its nutritional value, but also as a medicinal beverage, particularly for treatment of respiratory diseases.

The sheep was considered to be the most powerful animal and a symbol of life on earth. As for many peoples of the East, it also symbolized prosperity. The custom of slaughtering one for guests and the way it was divided up similarly had deep significance, each part of the sheep being served in a prescribed order of seniority.

The camel personified peace and prosperity. Besides its use as a beast of burden capable of carrying heavy loads, it was valued as source of camel hair and for its milk, considered the equal of mare's milk in its nutritional and medicinal properties. The Kazakhs mainly bred the more hardy two-humped, hairy camel. The single-humped camel or dromedary, being less resistant to cold, was raised only in the southern provinces.

The cow was regarded as a symbol of the after-life, and beef was eaten very rarely—only at the big festivals and in years of famine.

In common with many of the peoples of the East, the Kazakhs' respect for animals is reflected in the calendar they use, where each year of a twelve-year cycle is named after a different animal.

Numerous archaeological finds testify to the exceptional variety and richness of the culture of the Kazakh nomads, which has left its imprint on the life of the Kazakh population today.

126. When formally dressed a Kazakh woman had to wear rings, earrings, bracelets, pendants and braid decorations, like these fashioned in silver.

184

*127. A pectoral
ornament of the type
worn by girls for
special occasions.*

185

128. *A woman's ring and an ornamental brooch or plaque which was attached to a belt. Silver was the metal most widely used for jewelry.*

129. *Details of women's belts. These were made of leather, velvet and silk and decorated with hammered or engraved plaques.*

130. *A bracelet would often be attached to rings with fine chains, emphasizing the beauty of the woman's hands.*

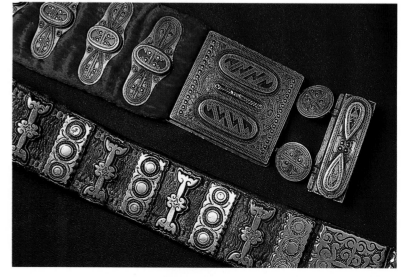

131, 132. Massive silver bracelets of this type were made by the craftsmen of western Kazakhstan and are characteristic of this region.

133-135, 137, 138. The head-dresses worn by girls had to have additional long pendants attached to the sides. These were made of small silver, sometimes gilt, plaques, strings of pearls, semi-precious stones, coins or silk thread, variously combined. The length and number of the pendants was a mark of the parents' prosperity.

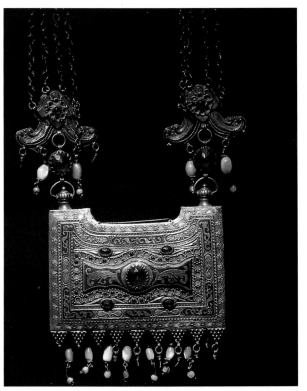

138. A fine horse with a beautiful and expensive saddle and other accoutrements indicated the nomad's worth and social position, so that much time and skill was put into the making of these objects. In the picture above: a Kazakh saddle and man's belt.

*139, 140. Details of ornaments and
jewelry. Bracelets and rings, with or
without stones, were worn by both young
and older women. They were decorated
with a variety of techniques: filigree
work, granulation, appliqué, engraving
and stamping.*

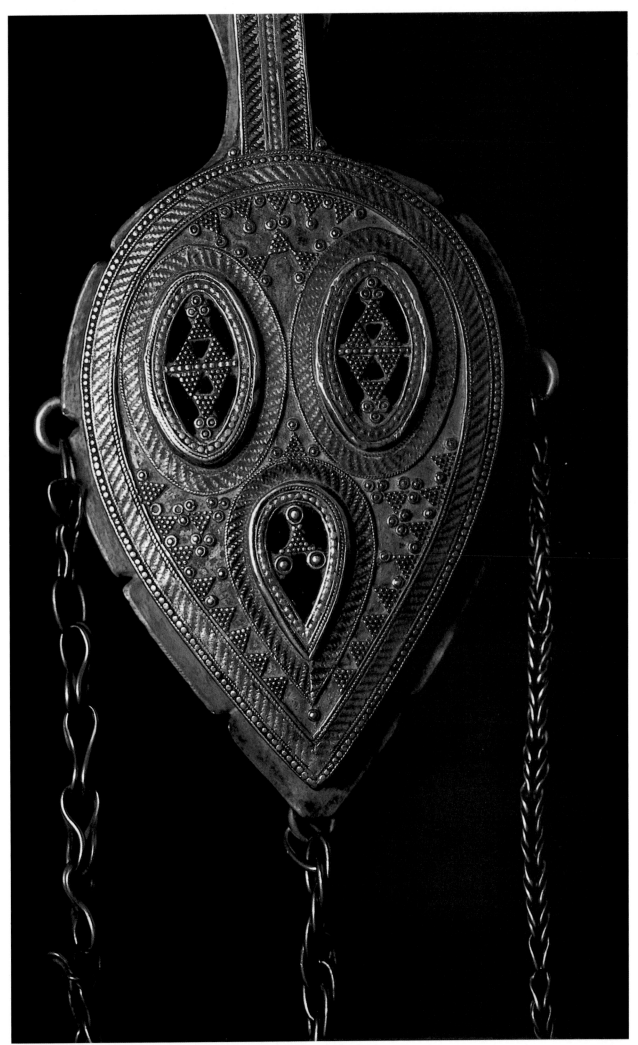

193

141. A pectoral ornament. Such pendants could be rectangular plaques, small triangular boxes or hollow tubes, decorated with engraving, niello and granulation, and studded with semi-precious stones and gems.

194

142. The craftsmen of Kazakhstan
showed astonishing imagination and
skill in combining motifs and materials
to produce an endless variety of
jewelry and personal ornaments.
Above, rings for two fingers.

143, 144. The large range of traditional musical instruments includes various pipes and the 'kobyz', a stringed instrument played like a 'cello.

196

*145-149. The Kazakhs are an
exceptionally musical people. In the
absence of a written literature or
representational art, in the past they
found their artistic expression
primarily in music, which accompanied
the nomads throughout their lives, from
birth to death. The examples pictured
here are displayed in the Museum of
Musical Instruments in Almaty.*

150, 151. Folk music instruments are to be found in almost every family, and children are taught to play them at an early age.

152, 153. The two-stringed 'dombra' is one of the most popular of the folk instruments. Here is it pictured against traditional Kazakh carpets.

154. Girls dress up for national festivals in finery they borrow from their grand-mothers' chests.

155. Festivals are always accompanied by theatrical performances where the deeds of the old warriors are celebrated by actors in authentic costumes.

156. Examples of fine Kazakh weaving and needlecraft. The broad bands served both to decorate the yurt and bind together its structural parts.

157. The craft of making the ancient musical instruments is often passed down in families from one generation to the next.

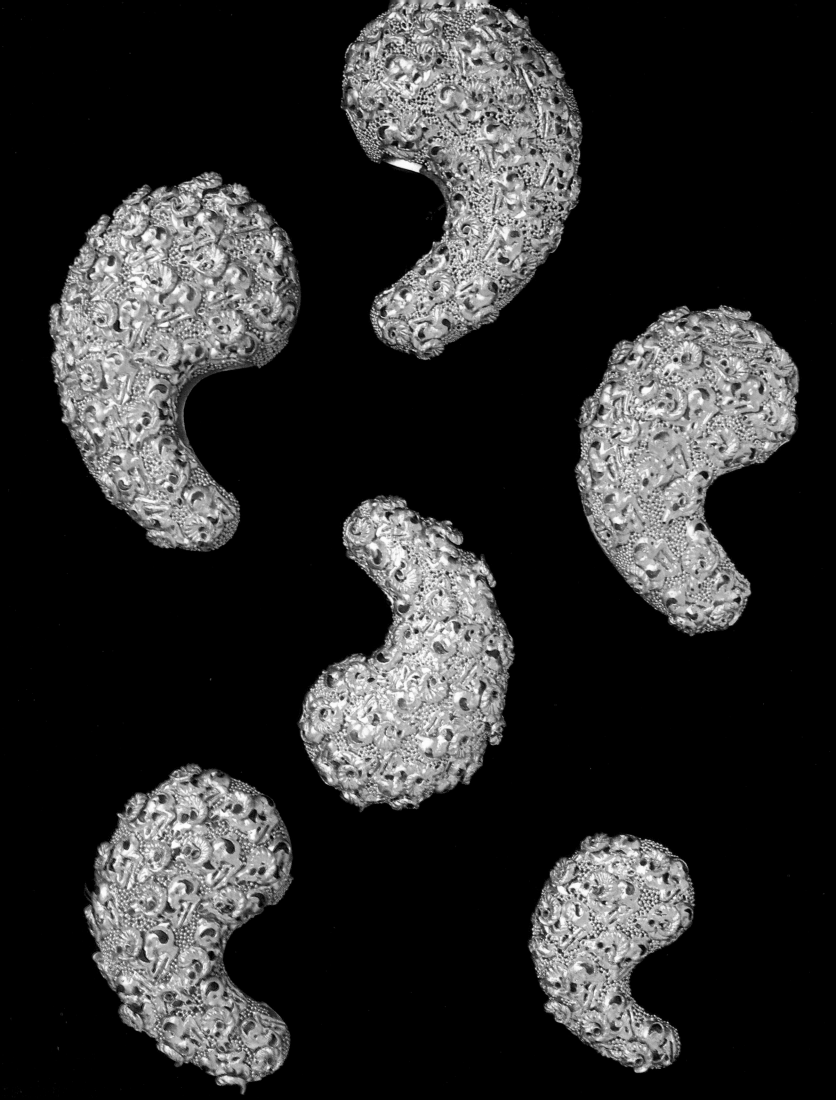

The Family

Childhood. One of the most important events in the Kazakh family was and remains the birth of a baby. It must be admitted that the joy of this event is doubled if a son is born. The genealogy of the Kazakhs passes down the male line. Offspring are considered to be grandchildren only when they are born into the family of a son. The children of a daughter are not regarded as grandchildren, but they enjoy specially warm treatment from the parents and relations on the mother's side. Birth, the first bath, laying in the cradle, the first steps, the ritual of circumcision, being put on a horse for the first time—all these events in the life of the child were occasions for a celebration, a remarkable event in the family, the aul and the clan, often accompanied by lavish entertainment with horse races, contests of singers and musicians, games and amusements.

The child in the traditional Kazakh family knew no restrictions and could do as it liked up to the age of seven. It was considered that before this age, a child was not a reasonable being, but at seven it became a personality with a will. The Kazakhs believed that the basic education should be given from the age of seven to twelve, after which it was too late, and that the formation of a person's physical, mental and sensible faculties was completed at the age of twenty-five.

Marriage. The next major step in life is marriage. To marry off a son, the father would first send close relatives to the family of the prospective bride to enter into negotiations. If the girl and her relations were not opposed to the union, both sides decided on a date. For the official betrothal, the father of the bridegroom sent close relations, or even went himself, to the parents of the bride. At this stage, the bride price and the time of the wedding would be discussed. Both sides took an oath, which was sealed by the visitors dipping the thumbs of their right hands in a cup of blood of a freshly slaughtered sheep. In earlier times the oath was confirmed by dipping the tips of their spears and arrows in a cup of blood. After the oath, the elders of the clan ratified the betrothal and both sides ate from one plate a dish of liver and sheep's fat, symbolizing the kinship and prosperity of both families. The ritual was completed with the presentation of gifts to the parents of the bride.

After this, the future bridegroom paid his first visit to his betrothed, bringing a part of the bride price, valuable gifts and what was necessary for the wedding ceremony: rings, earrings, bracelets, silks and furs. A special yurt was made ready for the bridegroom and those accompanying him, and a celebration was arranged. On the following day the women of the aul introduced the bride and groom. After this visit, the parties started preparing for the wedding day. The father of the groom was responsible for the bride price, the entertainment at the wedding and gifts for the bride's relatives. Her brothers and other close relatives were presented with various gifts: a swift horse, a hunting bird, a silver saddle and accoutrements, gold and silver bars and coins.

When he went to fetch the bride, the bridegroom was accompanied by his mother and a group of friends and relatives. Especial respect was shown to the mother of the bride, because she had suckled the daughter.

The wedding rites started off in the aul of the bride. A few days before her send-off, the bride had said farewell to her relatives and neighbours. Accompanied by her sisters-in-law and other brides, she would go into each dwelling to receive blessings and gifts. As she left

158. The National Museum has many valuable archaeological finds, such as these golden ornaments from a Sak treasure trove.

her parents' home, she sang the farewell song—the *synsu*.

When the wedding procession reached the bridegroom's aul, girls and young women would help the bride to dismount from her horse and lead her into the aul, where she was greeted with the traditional song—the *betashar*, which literally means 'the revealing of the face' of the bride. The bridegroom's mother would greet the bride as soon as she stepped across the threshold, which she had to do with her right foot first, to ensure that she would bring prosperity to the family and would be happy in her new home. The mother then poured a spoon of oil on the fire, held her hands over the flame, and then passed them over the face of the bride.

The Elderly. The Kazakhs have always honoured age. Grandmothers and grandfathers are practically the heads of the family, and enjoy the respect and love of the household. Indeed, the everyday life of the family revolves round the well-being of the elderly. The moral level and material well-being of the family as a whole are measured by the position of the old people.

The cult of ancestors entails honouring the memory of those who have passed on, the preservation of the family hearth and the continuation of the family. Originating in the distant past, it was a guarantee of the preservation of the people and their ethnic integrity. Every Kazakh had to know his family tree to the seventh generation. When Kazakhs met each other, one of the first things was to find out if the other person knew his forefathers to the seventh generation. Even a seven-year-old child had to know the answer to this question. Not to know one's origins was considered a sign of having been badly brought up.

The Woman's Role. The Kazakh woman was expected to show great respect for her husband's family, never daring to contradict her parents-in-law. She would try to keep out of sight of her husband's father or elder brothers, and did not presume to utter their names, even when they were absent. She called the younger brothers and sisters by names that had been thought up.

The women bore the brunt of the work connected with the hearth, the aged and the children. The moral and spiritual well-being not only of the family, but also of the aul and the whole clan, depended to a great extent on the women, who bore many burdens and were tireless workers.

Though surrounded by prohibitions and restrictions, the Kazakh woman never covered her face and was not without rights. She was never left to fend for herself; parental care in childhood was later replaced by that of her husband and, in her old age, of grown-up sons. Every clan or tribe, not to mention close relatives, felt obliged to care for a widow. If a marriage broke down, a rarity in the past, the rights and interests of the wife were protected in the first place. Important family matters were never decided in the absence of the women, and their wishes and demands were always taken into consideration. Women sat at table in their own right and not just as a decoration. The Kazakh woman was not only a caring wife and mother, a kind and generous head of the household, but as an equal of the men she would also mount a horse and take up arms against enemies. Her wisdom and beauty, femininity and bravery, eloquence and resourcefulness, have been celebrated by poets through the ages and are recounted in legends and stories.

Hospitality. The laws of hospitality were strictly observed in the steppe. Guests were classified as invited and uninvited—guests sent by

God', that is, travellers. The traveller had the right to stay in any yurt, regardless of whether or not he knew the owner. He was certain that he would be accepted in any yurt with respect and be given refreshments, a bed and fodder for his horse. He was free to stay as long as he needed. He even had the right to demand better treatment if he was not satisfied with his reception as a guest. According to *Adat*, the Muslim law, the guest enjoyed the full protection of the host of the yurt while he was staying under his roof. The host was bound, if such circumstances arose, to defend his guest from enemies.

It was considered impolite and a breach of the law of hospitality to subject the guest to questioning before he had quenched his thirst and been fed. But it was another matter if the guest himself wanted to be forthcoming. The guest had the best place in the home and the best treatment.

Burial. As far as funeral rites were concerned, the people attached great significance to the tradition of informing relatives of the death of a near one with verses of consolation. There are many examples of this type of comforting oration, which demanded great artistic inventiveness. In these verses, tribute was paid to the qualities of the dead person and his place in society, while the relatives were called upon to be strong in their misfortune, and were wished health and prosperity.

According to ancient custom, the women of the family lamented over the dead person for a long time and observed strict mourning for a year. The deceased was laid out on the right side of the yurt, or if he was a man of substance in a special mourning yurt. Its floor would be covered with rugs, and there would be a bed on the right side, covered with a black rug, on which the body would remain till the end of the ceremony of leave-taking. The deceased would then be carried out of the home feet first, thus underlining that he was leaving forever.

It was traditional to attach a cloth on the end of a lance on the top right-hand side of the dead person's yurt, as a mark of honouring and mourning the dead. The colour of the banner could be black, white, red or striped, depending on the position and age of the departed.

Funeral feasts were held on the seventh and fortieth days after death, and a year later. At the funeral feasts of the most respected people, apart from refreshments, races and wrestling were organized, with rich prizes for the winners.

The Kazakh respect for the memory of the dead had some distinctive aspects. According to an ancient tradition, no physical reminder should be left of those whose bodies had been committed to the earth, and so gravestones were rarely erected. Later, mausoleums, stone stelae and tombstones were erected only on the graves of Muslim saints and persons especially revered among the people. However, at the end of the eighteenth century, monuments did begin to be erected over the graves of the more prosperous inhabitants of the steppe, and well-to-do people built family burial vaults.

The Food of the Nomad

The Kazakhs' traditional diet depended on their basic economic activities: herding and arable farming, and consisted almost exclusively of what they produced themselves: milk, meat, grains and other plants. In many respects this dietary pattern is still followed by the Kazakhs of today.

They consume a great variety and quantity of dairy food. All possible types of yoghurt and sour-milk products are made from the milk of sheep, goats and cows, as well as many kinds of dried cheese, which can be preserved for a long time and are highly calorific. There are also sweetmeats made of milk beverages to which millet, wheat or rice are added. Mare's milk, *koumiss*, specially prepared in a wooden bowl, is highly valued for its nutritional and medicinal properties. In the same way a drink called *shubat* is made from camel's milk. Today, these beverages are used effectively in the treatment of various illnesses in modern medical institutions.

Meat also figured largely in the nomad's diet. There was a plentiful supply from domesticated animals: sheep, goats, camels and large-horned cattle, and also from wild sheep, elik (hornless small deer), steppe antelope and other animals caught by hunting. A special place in the Kazakh cuisine belongs today, as it did in the past, to horse meat, which calls for very careful cooking. From this, many types of sausage and various other delicacies are made. Horse meat, smoked and dried, is usually prepared for the winter. Fish is also eaten. In the southern regions there is a higher consumption of fruit and vegetables.

A great variety of dishes and many types of bread are made from cereals, particularly wheat, millet and rice. Grain is first boiled, then roasted and crushed in a mortar, after which creamy butter and sugar are added. These and various milk-based sweets take the place of other types of confectionery.

One of the favourite drinks of the Kazakhs is tea. The black varieties are drunk with or without milk. In the southern regions green tea is popular. In the past the Kazakhs had no alcoholic beverages.

The cuisine of the modern Kazakh is much more varied, since it has assimilated the traditions of many peoples. Certain Kazakh national dishes are now prepared only for holidays or special celebrations.

The dishes and utensils used in bygone centuries for the serving and preparation of food were very varied in form, size and purpose. Vessels for keeping sour-milk products were made from specially worked leather. Wooden plates and dishes could be richly ornamented, inset with silver and bone. Earthenware pitchers, pots and cups were often glazed or painted. Porcelain, faience and metal plates and dishes were also in use.

Traditional Dress

The Kazakh national costume is a unique manifestation of the material culture of the past. Its forms were suited to conditions of life on the steppe: its very hot summers, strong winds and the bitter cold of winter. Clothing was made of woollen, cotton, silk or velvet fabrics, and outer garments were usually made of or lined with fur.

The men wore shirts, quilted jackets, tunics and a distinctive long, loose coat: the *chapan*. Winter clothing consisted of quilted garments with an interlining of camel hair or sheep's wool, coats of fur or of leather with the fleece inside, and on top of these wide cloaks made of thick, impermeable cloth. For winter their wide trousers were sewn from leather with the fleece inside, and for summer from either goat hide or steppe antelope hide without fur.

The headwear of Kazakh men was a sharply pointed hat, trimmed with fox-fur, sable or mink. In the summer these were replaced by tall caps of thin felt. The typical footwear of the nomad was boots which widened above the knees, with high heels, and in summer light, soft boots with a curled toe (*ichigs*) or sandals.

The quality and ornamentation of a woman's clothes reflected her position in society. Unmarried girls wore conical hats trimmed with fur and decorated with eagle-owl feathers, or small hats ornamented with beads, pearls and precious stones. Dresses made of silk, cotton or velvet were worn under a bodice, tunic or sleeveless jacket of woollen cloth or velvet. Their borders were often richly ornamented with embroidery in gold or silver thread, lace, brocade or beads. Over the tunic or jacket they wore a velvet or leather belt with silver clasps and decorative plaques. Their light leather boots were embroidered with coloured thread and encrusted with silver decorative motifs. In summer these were replaced by high-heeled shoes or sandals. For ceremonial occasions, they had boots of green leather, decorated with embroidered patterns and silver.

Older women wore jackets or tunics, usually with sleeves, over free-flowing dresses, and on their heads a large kerchief or shawl wound around in various ways (the *kimeshek*, *jaulyk*, *sulama*), which covered the hair and shoulders and fell down the back. In the colder seasons their dress consisted of warm, quilted, velvet garments and fur coats, the type of fur being a measure of the wealth of the wearer.

Another garment was the *beldemshe*, a full, wrap-around skirt of velvet or thin cloth, which was gathered at the waist on a wide belt of the same material, fastened with buttons or a buckle.

A very ancient type of headwear was the pill-box shaped *kasaba*, made out of velvet embroidered with gold, and lavishly decorated with beads and pendants, with coral, turquoise and other semi-precious stones, gems and discs resembling coins. Sometimes a feather was added at the front, where there would be longer pendants. Married women wore the *kasaba* without feathers, and added a kerchief. As further adornment, women wore necklaces, earrings, bracelets, rings, pendants for the hair and filigree belts.

Children's clothes were basically smaller-scale versions of those worn by adults, though less elaborately ornamented.

The everyday dress of the modern Kazakh is westernized and differs little from that of other peoples, though national costume, or elements of it, are proudly worn on festive occasions.

LIFE TODAY

Independent Kazakhstan

The young sovereign state and its economy have set out on a new course in which the social organism and the whole complex of political and economic relations are being completely reorganized. The development of democracy, new property-ownership relations, and the steady move towards a market economy are creating favourable conditions for the emergence of a strong national state. As reality demands, the society and economy are more and more assuming an open character. But at the same time it is vital to take into account the traditions and psychology of the people, as well as the negative effects of the totalitarian regime on the mentality and attitudes of the population, which to some extent are nowadays obstacles in the way of change and more rapid progress.

The President of the Republic, Nursultan Nazarbaev, defining the strategy of Kazakhstan's development, said:

'Fate has decreed that the time of difficult decisions on the radical re-organization of life should fall to our lot. The totalitarian society created over many years by the Communist regime collapsed literally before our eyes, and without any tangible outside pressure. The main reason for this lay in the fact that...from the very beginning in the former USSR, the Soviet people never really felt that they were the true masters of their lives, their property, their country, but merely dumb cogs in the party-state machine.'

These honest words of President Nursultan Nazarbaev expose the real essence of Soviet Russian imperialism.

Independent Kazakhstan has a precise conception of how its society should develop and is striving to instil confidence among its people to achieve the ideals and lofty dreams, setting itself concrete strategic goals which find expression in the founding of a strong presidential republic, based on the interests of the indigenous nation: the Kazakhs. Remembering that the policy of denationalization of the Soviet period brought the Kazakh nation to the brink of catastrophe and extinction, the government is paying serious attention to the revival of the national culture and language, and to the renewal of spiritual and cultural ties with the Kazakh diaspora, forced to leave Kazakhstan at various times in the past century.

The multi-party system is the decisive force in the democratic transformation and consolidation of the multinational society. The adoption of such a system will lead to the emergence of new political activists and leaders.

The most important political aims, and the main condition for the realization of economic reforms, are the preservation of stability in the country and the conclusion of military, political and economic alliances that will guarantee the security and the sovereignty of Kazakhstan,

The advantageous geopolitical position of Kazakhstan, facilitating trade and political ties with both Europe and Asia, can be used for linking Europe, the Central Asian part of the former USSR and other parts of Asia.

The country's internal tasks are closely related to the fact that for the first time in its recent history it has real conditions for all-round development, for the rebirth of the Kazakh nation and other nationalities of the republic. The forging of social unity within the multi-ethnic society and success in rallying all the peoples of the republic for the general well-being will be a yardstick of the progress of Kazakhstan's statehood.

The Political System

The Constitution. The first Constitution of the independent Republic of Kazakhstan, promulgated in January 1993, is based on the principles of pluralism and separation of powers within a unified, secular state.

The highest legislative body in the country is the single-chamber Supreme Soviet, to which 360 members are elected for a five-year period. The deputies to the Supreme Soviet, the provincial councils and local government bodies, like the President of the Republic, are elected by direct, general suffrage by secret ballot.

The President. The President of the Republic is the head of state and chief executive. The Constitution lays down that no one can hold this office for more than two terms. The President exercises the powers vested in him by the Constitution by issuing decrees, orders and resolutions. He signs the laws of republican significance and has the right to return to the Supreme Soviet the text of a law submitted to him for further consideration and repeat voting. If the Supreme Soviet confirms its previous position by a majority of not less than two thirds of the votes, the President is obliged to sign the law. The President has the right to declare a state of emergency, temporarily curtailing rights and liberties. However, the decree must be approved by the Supreme Soviet, and for the duration of the state of emergency no changes can be made to the Constitution.

The President is assisted in his work by the Vice-President. With the agreement of the Supreme Soviet, the President appoints the Prime Minister, on whose recommendation the members of the Cabinet of Ministers are appointed.

The Constitutional Court. The Constitutional Court, the highest judicial body in the land, decides whether laws and decrees, and also international contacts and agreements which the republic enters into, are in accordance with the Constitution. The presiding judge and other judges who make up the Constitutional Court are chosen by the Supreme Soviet on the recommendation of the President of the Republic for a term of ten years. The judges are independent and subordinate only to the Constitution and the laws of the land.

If the President or the Chairman of the Supreme Soviet does not lodge an objection to a decision of the Constitutional Court, it comes into force immediately. If, following an objection, the decision is confirmed by the judges by a majority of no less than two thirds of the votes, it then comes into force. The judgements of the Constitutional Court are final and cannot be appealed against.

Political Parties. The Constitution of Kazakhstan guarantees the right of associations, parties and movements, with the exception of groups proved guilty of 'inciting racial, national, social or religious intolerance, or advocating the superiority of certain strata of society', and also those whose aim is to overthrow the Constitution. Apart from this, the activity of a political party cannot be based on religion, and religious organizations must not pursue political aims.

Regional and International Relations. Soon after its declaration of independence, Kazakhstan was officially recognized by more than 100 states. In 1993 the following countries had embassies or representation in Almaty: Afghanistan, Armenia, Canada, China, Cuba, Egypt, France, Georgia, Germany, Great Britain, Hungary, India, Iran, Italy, Japan, South Korea, Switzerland, Tadzhikistan, Turkey, USA and Uzbekistan. Diplomatic relations have been established with many other states, the majority of which have an ambassador to the

Community of Independent States (CIS) in Moscow. Kazakhstan is a member of many different international organizations, including the Council for Security and Co-operation in Europe, the United Nations Organisation, the International Monetary Fund, the World Bank, the European Bank for Reconstruction and Development, the Asian Development Bank and Organisation of Economic Co-operation, which unites Afghanistan, Azerbaijan, the countries of Central Asia, Iran, Pakistan and Turkey. In 1992 Kazakhstan concluded an agreement on technical co-operation with the European Union, which has representation in Almaty.

The Economy

The economy of Kazakhstan, like that of all the former republics of the USSR, is passing through a very complex and critical phase. The legacy of the inefficient old system and the dependence on processes occurring in the Russian economy continue to exert a strong influence on the economic development of Kazakhstan.

The republic's economy is characterized by two features: first, the transition from a centralized planned economy with an out-of-date structure and technology to a market economy; and, second, the exisiting infrastructure created to satisfy the needs of the former USSR and not the market within the republic.

The reforms that are being carried out are designed on the model of western economies, taking into account the country's great mineral wealth and the development of industry based on its exploitation, and also the country's extensive agricultural land. Together, these provide the preconditions for the development of a diversified economy.

Agriculture. Kazakhstan had over 20 per cent of the agricultural land of the Soviet Union. In grain production, it occupied third place, after Russia and the Ukraine. The annual consumption of 16 to 17 million tons leaves significant quantities for export in years of good harvest. In 1992-93 the republic was fifth in the world in the export of grain, after the USA, the European Union, Canada and Australia.

Nearly 82 per cent of the republic's territory is used for farming, of which 15 per cent is arable land. Large areas of the low hill land in north and north-western Kazakhstan were ploughed up in the campaign to open up the virgin land.

Mixed farming is practised in the mountainous and foothill regions, both with and without the use of irrigation. The large artificial lakes and canals that have been constructed, such as the Kapchagay, Chardaryn and Arys-Turkestan reservoirs and the Volga-Ural Canal, have been of great benefit to agriculture.

The government's economic development programme envisages a rational and radical reform of the agro-industrial complexes, and measures to ensure the satisfactory supply of the market. The programme will promote the economic revival of rural areas. The privatization of agricultural production is in progress, and the legal basis for long-term leasing of land has been created.

Industry. Industry is the leading sector of the economy. Between 1989 and 1993 there was a sharp fall in industrial production, despite the fact that the share of industry in the national revenue rose from 30 per cent to 40 per cent. Industry is oriented towards the utilization of the country's own raw material resources, with mining, chemicals and metallurgy as the major branches.Engineering, light industry and food

159. The single-minaret mosque in Semipalatinsk, built at the end of the nineteenth century.

160. Imam of a mosque in Semipalatinsk. As the role of religion in society increases, so does the respect accorded its representatives.

161. Interior of the prayer hall of the two-minaret mosque in Semipalatinsk.

processing are other important sectors.

Energy. Electric power in Kazakhstan comes from two independent networks. In the north the electric power system is linked with the grid in Russia, and in the south with the grid of the republics of Central Asia. Kazakhstan exports electricity, but at the same time it is necessary to import thirty per cent of the required electric power.

The programme for the development of electricity production in the republic provides for an increase in the number of gas-powered stations. At present there are only five of these; about 80 per cent of electricity is produced by 54 coal-powered stations. The only nuclear-powered station is located on the shore of the Caspian Sea.

Oil. Kazakhstan's known oil resources amount to 2.9 milliard tons. Most of these reserves are concentrated in comparatively few deposits, of which the ten main ones account for about 90 per cent. Taking into consideration the low level of prospecting in the past, it can be assumed that not all the deposits of oil have been discovered.

In March 1993 the state-owned Kazakhstan-Caspian Shelf Company was set up to manage and control all exploratory work and extraction of oil and gas in the region of the Caspian Sea belonging to Kazakhstan, covering an area of 103,000 square kilometres. A consortium consisting of Agip, British Gas, BP/State Oil, and the Mobil, Shell and Total companies signed a preparatory agreement to undertake exploratory work in the region. The Kazakhstan-Caspian Shelf Company expects exploratory drilling to start in 1997, and the extraction of oil in the year 2000.

There are no reliable estimates of the country's potential oil resources, but preparatory data indicate that, even by the most conservative calculations, they are double the present known reserves, which would place the republic on a level with Russia in this respect. According to the more optimistic evaluations, Kazakhstan has an amount equivalent to 85 per cent of the known oil reserves of Kuwait.

It is also estimated that the country possesses two trillion cubic metres of natural gas, which is double the level of the present known reserves. The effective extraction of these supplies demands the use of advanced technology and equipment and a huge capital outlay. The cost of exploration of the deposits is estimated at nearly 200 million US dollars, while the cost of extraction may reach 30 milliard dollars.

The biggest deal between Kazakhstan and a leading oil company was concluded in April 1993, when Chevroil and Kazakhstan founded a combined enterprise for exploration and extraction of oil, called TengizChevroil. The agreement, which is valid for forty years, envisages that within ten years the republic will become a leading oil exporter. The combined enterprise, which will exploit the oil deposits of Tengiz and Korolevsk, should increase the yearly output of these two deposits from 3.25 million tons at present to 35 million tons in 2007. When the TengizChevroil project is fully operational, it plans to extract from six to nine milliard barrels.

Deals on oil and gas have also been concluded with some other companies, such as Elf, British Gas and the Turkish companies BMB and Turkiye Petrolleri, and also with the sultanate of Oman. It is a complicated picture, but the government, together with foreign companies, plans the exploitation of more than forty oil fields. Towards the year 2000, on the basis of agreed contacts, the export of oil could reach a level three times higher than in 1994, and bring in up to three milliard dollars a year.

174. The Orthodox Cathedral in Almaty, an interesting wooden building in an astonishing mixture of styles, dating from 1907. Formerly used as a museum, it is now open for worship again.

The existing infrastructure is inadequate for the planned oil and gas ventures and the amount of oil which the country is intending to put on the world market. The improvement and broadening of this infrastructure demand a gigantic capital outlay. Since Kazakhstan has no direct outlet to the sea, the oil must be transported across the territory of other states, a fact that presents additional difficulties of access to the world market.

At the present time, oil from Kazakhstan has to be sent through the Russian system of pipelines, either to the Black Sea or to Europe. The only alternative is the use of relatively small-capacity barges to transport oil across the Caspian Sea. These conditions, which did not satisfy the country's needs, were aggravated after Russia decreased Kazakhstan's pipeline quota, resulting in a fall in production.

Many alternative ways of transporting Kazakh oil to the world market are at present in various stages of planning and construction. The variants include a pipeline through Russia (along the northern shore of the Caspian) to Novorossisk, a pipeline through Turkmenistan to Iran, and a sea transport route from Aktau to Iran. But even these alternatives present difficulties. Turkey, for instance, recently announced its intention to review the 1936 Montreuil Convention on unimpeded passage of cargo vessels through the Bosphorus straits—precisely the route that tankers use for shipping oil from Novorossisk.

Within Kazakhstan, it is planned to build a pipeline to link the west of the country with the oil refineries located in Pavlodar and Shimkent. Both towns are already joined by pipelines to the oil fields of Siberia. Plans have been announced to increase the capacity of existing oil refineries and build new ones. At present 184,000 barrels can be refined daily, a figure that the government aims to increase to 800,000 by the year 2000.

Gas. The gas industry is another branch that has great potential. The republic consumes 16 to 18 milliard cubic metres annually, while present production is not above 7 to 8 milliard. The shortfall is covered by importing from Uzbekistan, Turkmenistan and Russia. Projected calculations indicate that by the end of the decade, the country's gas requirements will reach 28 milliard cubic metres. The main gas field now being exploited is located in Karachaganak, and is one of the biggest in the world, with estimated reserves of 566 milliard cubic metres. Because of its proximity to the Russian Orenburg gas field and its insufficient processing capacities, the output of this field is at present exported to Russia. It is hoped that the extraction of gas will increase significantly as a result of works being carried out in the region by British Gas and Agip under a contract with Kazakhstan.

Coal. According to the figures for 1993, the republic was the tenth largest producer of coal in the world. Most of the coal it exports goes to Russia. However, since 1988 output has been falling as a result of the decline in demand on Kazakhstan's traditional export markets and the difficulties arising from the use of outdated technology and the decreasing yields of certain mines. According to prognoses, the cleaner types of fuel derived from coal will take its place on the internal market at competitive prices, thus enabling the coal mining industry to develop. In Kazakhstan there are deposits of types of coal that can be used in chemicals production, but this potential remains untapped as yet.

Minerals. Kazakhstan is justly called 'a subterranean treasure trove'. Over 90 per cent of all the minerals known on earth are found in the country and almost all the elements in the Mendelev table are

extracted here. More than 2,000 commercially exploitable deposits are known at present. Some 90 per cent of the chromite reserves of the former USSR are found in the republic, almost half the reserves of tungsten and lead, 40 per cent of the reserves of zinc and copper, and a quarter of the reserves of bauxite, phosphorus and silver. It possesses more than half of the world's known reserves of chrome, and takes third place in world reserves of manganese.

In 1993 the extraction of copper ore reached 300,000 tons, making up three per cent of the world total, while the production of refined copper, which is carried on in the Jezkazgan foundry, reached 370,000 tons.

Some 100,000 tons of lead ore were extracted, equivalent to 3.5 per cent of world production. The output of refined lead is at the moment 280,000 tons. All Kazakhstan's lead is smelted at the Ust-Kamenogorsk lead-zinc refinery, the most important copper-smelting plant of the former Soviet Union. Lead extraction in the republic accounts for 70 per cent of the total for the whole CIS, and the export of Kazakhstan lead to this region comprises 56,000 tons. The production of zinc in 1992 reached 265,000 tons, which comprised 40 per cent of the total output of the CIS and 3.5 per cent of world production.

Kazakhstan took third place in the production of gold in the former USSR. Although 173 deposits have been found, the majority are not worked; most of the gold is obtained as a by-product of copper and zinc mining. In view of the decline in the extraction of gold in the republic, the government recently announced a programme to achieve a fourfold increase in 1997. Apart from this, many other projects to develop gold mining are at an advanced stage. The Bakyrchi mine, located in the north-east, has estimated reserves of eight million ounces. At present 600 tons of silver are refined as a by-product of the extraction of non-ferrous ores.

Uranium is mined at three main deposits: near Stepnogorsk in northern Kazakhstan, not far from the town of Aktau in the west of the country and in the region of the town of Taboshar in the south. The republic extracted 55 per cent of all uranium in the former USSR. Kazakhstan's uranium producers and two Canadian firms have jointly formed the Catep Company, which is to invest nearly three million dollars in the production of uranium in the republic. These Canadian firms will also act as agents for the sale of uranium on the world market.

Kazakhstan is one of the most important producers of chromite in the CIS. The extraction of titanium ore comprises 40 per cent. This metal is used in aeroplane manufacture, the making of sputniks and chemical equipment. The Ulbin metallurgical factory produces an average of 300,000 tons of tantalum a year. Beryllium, which is resistant to corrosion, is used in the nuclear industry, electronics, space research and the defence industry.

Infrastructure. The economy of Kazakhstan until recently was oriented to the needs of the former Soviet Union. A factor that had a major impact on its development, and especially on its transport links, was the existence in the republic of deposits of various strategic materials, as a result of which travel was restricted on a significant part of its territory. In consequence, until quite recently the land-locked republic had few direct contacts with territories outside the Soviet Union. One of the priorities for Kazakhstan at present is the establishment of international ties, along with the expansion and modernization of its communications.

The first railway linking Kazakhstan with China is already operating, and another railway is being built to connect Kazakhstan with Iran and Turkey through Uzbekistan and Turkmenistan. The airport of Almaty, which in the Soviet period was intended only for internal flights, is now being enlarged. Already many international airlines fly into Almaty. A new airport will be built in the town of Aktau on the shore of the Caspian. Projects are being prepared to increase the capacity of ports on the Caspian Sea, and also to build Kazakhstan's own fleet. From the Caspian, ships could reach the main urban and industrial centres in the west of Russia, and also the Baltic and Black seas, using the Volga and its tributaries and canals.

Public Health

The decades preceding the collapse of the USSR were marked by the intensification of negative processes in the social milieu, as well as in the economy. The legacy of the former system of financing has contributed to the slow progress in the improvement of the health service, education and pre-school institutions. People's health and the quality of life are directly dependent on the condition of the natural environment. The policy of intensive industrialization, particularly the building of gigantic industrial and power complexes, as well as the proliferation of military sites, brought about a significant deterioration in the environment. An extremely serious ecological situation has developed in the Aral Sea region, where the excessive diversion of water from the rivers Amu Darya and Syr Darya to irrigate the cotton fields has lowered the water level of this great inland salt lake by 15 metres and reduced the volume of water by 54 per cent. The shore line has receded in the south and east by 60 to 120 kilometres, leaving 25,000 square kilometres of dry sea bed, from which an estimated 25 million tons of sand, dust and salt rise annually into the atmosphere. The drying up of the Aral Sea, coupled with the chemical pollution of its waters, has had a devastating effect on the ecology and sanitary-epidemiological conditions of the region.

A no less alarming ecological situation has developed in the area of the Semipalatinsk (Semey) nuclear testing ground, where 470 surface explosions have been carried out. Towns and villages with non-ferrous metal works and chemical production are likewise exposed to a dangerously high level of environmental pollution.

All this has had an alarming effect on demographic trends and the public health: the birth rate has declined by six per cent, while the general mortality rate has risen by more than 13.6 per cent, resulting in the slowing down of the natural growth of the population. The mortality rate among infants and mothers continues to rise. The incidence of infectious diseases has sharply increased, backwardness in the physical development of children and young persons is more common, the level of invalidity at a young age is high. More than 20 per cent of children are born with physical and mental defects. The number of cases of malignant diseases remains high, and in every fifth patient the diagnosis is not made until an advanced stage of the illness, primarily because of the shortage of adequate diagnostic equipment.

One of the basic reasons for the decline in the health of the population is the reduction in real terms in the financing of the whole public health system. Its institutions are short of medicines and other medical supplies, and lack of funds makes it impossible to acquire new medical equipment, technology and ambulances.

The system of public health is based on a ramified network of out-patient polyclinics and hospitals. There are 3,180 out-patient institutions, 24 medical research centres and six teaching institutes. Over 58,000 doctors, and 4,000 research and teaching scientific staff are employed. The level of provision of skilled medical staff is one of the highest in the countries of the CIS.

Under the conditions of the transition to a market economy, the Ministry of Public Health has adopted a programme of basic targeted reforms in the public health system and taken urgent measures to overcome the crisis. The Law on the Protection of Public Health in the Republic of Kazakhstan lays down the direction of development and defines the legal basis of this sector. In 1993 the government adopted a resolution on the introduction of medical insurance, which enabled the Ministry of Public Health to begin the experimental introduction of medical insurance in certain provinces of Kazakhstan, although the Law on Medical Insurance had not yet been passed. A series of normative documents have been prepared for this, and a uniform method of pricing medical services as well as the standards of provision of medical aid in all fields have been worked out.

Education

During the years of Soviet power, Kazakhstan acquired an education system that had a vertical structure of administration and was fully financed by the government. The duration of each phase of schooling is fixed, and when each is completed, a certificate or degree is awarded. Students are paid a stipend depending on their success, and teachers' earnings are related to their duties, experience and qualifications.

Children begin school at the age of six and have eight years of compulsory education. At the primary level they attend school for eight or ten years. After eight years they can enrol in a secondary vocational school, lasting two or three years, after which they are qualified to take up skilled employment or continue their education. Those who spend ten years in the primary-level school can enrol directly in an institution of higher education.

The plan of enrolment and graduation of specialists is drawn up by the state on the basis of the teaching requirements of the regions and the needs of various sectors of the national economy.

Under the conditions of a planned economy, the close relationship between the state and educational institutions was justified. The failings of such an educational system lay in tendencies towards the passive reception of knowledge, the orientation towards the 'average school-leaver' and the lack of correspondence between the requirements of society and the level and type of education of specialists.

The reforms in the education system now being prepared in the republic are based on its democratization in the sense of greater freedom of choice. The Law on Education makes provision for pre-school, primary and general secondary education, secondary vocational education, higher education and post-graduate studies. In addition to the state system of education, private secondary schools of a new type have appeared (variously called gymnasium, lycée or college).

There are three universities, two in Almaty and one in Karagandy. Regional universities are being founded in provincial capitals. Instead of traditional entrance exams, a new complex testing system is being introduced. Conditions are being established for inclusion in the world education system.

One of the main reasons for delaying *perestroika* in the field of education in Kazakhstan is financial. Kazakhstan lags behind the developed countries in the level of investment in education. The republic spends twelve times less per pupil and student than the United States, and eight times less than Great Britain.

The sovereign state of Kazakhstan needs an internationally oriented policy in the field of education and science. Integration into the world community cannot be achieved without harmonization of the educational systems. Little progress can be made in this field without taking into consideration the experience gained in the world, without direct contacts and the exchange of students and schoolchildren.

Joint education institutions and cultural-educational centres have been formed within the framework of international agreements: the Kazakh-Turkish International University has been founded in the town of Turkestan and 19 Kazakh-Turkish lyceés have been opened in 12 provinces of the republic; the Kazakh-German Academy of Economics, Law and Engineering is active in the town of Pavlodar, and a Kazakh-French college, France House, in Almaty.

Plans are also afoot to open a Kazakh-Egyptian academy, a Turkish language centre, a Kazakh-Chinese educational centre, and a Kazakh-Texas university in the city of Almaty.

The President of the Republic of Kazakhstan has set up an international fund, known as Bolashak, which allocates grants for the training of specialists abroad. In the last three years, 230 teachers of economics have had work experience in universities and major companies of the USA, France and Germany, while specialists from these countries and from Japan, China and Poland work in educational institutions in Kazakhstan.

The Ministry of Education follows the TEMPUS and TACI programmes of the European Union, directed at the reform of higher education and broadening ties between universities.

An agreement concluded with the Kinderdorf International organization makes provision for the building of children's villages in the

city of Almaty.

In 1994, 500,000 students were enrolled in the 248 vocational-technical schools, 63 institutes of higher education and universities, and 35 medical schools. In the 269 scientific-technical institutes, 26,000 scientific and technical staff are employed.

Sport

National games and pastimes of a sporting character were practised among the Kazakhs in the distant past. Early monuments and written sources bear witness not only to the tradition of the warrior, strong and agile, sharp-shooting and brave, ready to work and protect his homeland, but also to types of sport that have survived to this day. The most widespread and popular were wrestling (in the Kazakh style), horse racing and archery.

Hunting, important in the Kypchak economy, was not just a matter of catching prey for food and clothing, but also a form of military and physical training to develop will-power and character, strength and skill. The twelfth-century Jewish traveller Petakhya wrote that the Kypchaks were by nature 'exceptionally far-sighted, brilliant marksmen with the bow, who can kill birds on the wing'. Hunting demanded not only stamina and physical fitness, but also a knowledge of nature, of the habits of birds and beasts, and an ability to follow their tracks, as well as selfless readiness to come to the rescue or aid of a comrade.

During the hunt, the Kazakh became one with nature, shooting beasts and birds, but not damaging his surroundings. The most widespread forms of hunting were with beaters and with hunting birds: eagles, falcons and hawks. These were caught by various methods or taken as fledglings direct from their nests, which were usually on inaccessible mountain tops or sheer cliffs. Their taming and training demand great expertise, which has become a rarity in our day.

Hunting was the favourite entertainment of the khans, who would set off mounted on their best horse and wearing their finest clothes and armour. The departure for the hunt was a truly festive occasion. 'The nomad Turki are especially skilful and display exceptional endurance during the hunt. It is hard not to get highly excited watching them as they chase the wild goat or wild horse,' the Arab traveller al-Jakhiz wrote enthusiastically. Excellent marksmen enjoyed high esteem, and hunting was celebrated in poetry. The steppe people's constant companions and their pride were the fleet-footed horse and the proud hawk.

It can be said without exaggeration that in the past every able-bodied Kazakh male knew how to wrestle, learning the elements of the national style of wrestling in early childhood. At the beginning of this century in matches in Tokyo and Paris the celebrated *paluan* (wrestler) Hadji Mukan Munaytpasov won the title of absolute world champion. In Kazakhstan he was accorded the title of 'knight of the Kazakh people', an honour also given to the wrestler-poet Baluan Sholak.

Equestrian sports, without which no festival is complete, have always been widely popular. The first structure to be built for sports purposes in Kazakhstan was for equestrian competitions. This was the Almaty Hippodrome, built in 1911 and reconstructed in the 1930s and 1940s.

Since 1972 the high-mountain sports complex of Medeo has been famous for its speed-skating rink, where world championships in speed-skating are held and more than 100 world records have been broken. Medeo can take 17,000 spectators. A little higher than Medeo, at an altitude of 3,150 metres, is the skiing complex of Chinbulak. In 1980 at the Spartak Stadium the first cycling track was built.

Kazakhstan was represented by 65 sportsmen and women at the last Olympic Games. The names of Kazakh sportsmen and women are inscribed in the roll of world record-holders. Since independence, an Olympic centre has been built in Almaty, a significant investment aimed at promoting both top-level sport and a healthy life-style among the people.

The establishment of professional boxing in the republic owes most to Serik Konakbaev, winner of the World Cup, many times world champion and an Olympic silver medallist. The world wrestling champion Daulet Turlykhanov has created a private sporting complex where young people are trained in Greco-Roman wrestling and many types of eastern martial arts. The world champion in Tai Quando, Mustafa Ozturk, has also made an important contribution to the development of sport in Kazakhstan and the coaching of young people.

Tourism

Sporting activities are often closely interconnected with tourism, which began in Kazakhstan in the early twentieth century. In the 1930s guide-books on the tourist routes of Kazakhstan were written, and the first resorts were opened. The development of tourism was helped by the organization of mass mountain climbs to the summit of Mount Komsomol in the Zaili Alatau, the first of which took place in 1935.

Kazakhstan is a land of enormous contrasts: majestic mountain peaks clad in eternal snow, hot sandy deserts, densely forested massifs and the endless, rolling grasslands of the steppe. Here the traveller will find many enchanting areas of wild and unspoilt nature. One such region is Kokshetau province with its emerald lakes framed by extraordinary cliffs carved by the elements into fantastic shapes, its sandy beaches and pure air, fragrant with the scent of pine, offering wonderful conditions for rest and relaxation.

The lakes of Jasybay and Sabyndykol in northern Kazakhstan capture the imagination with their fabled beauty. The awe-inspiring crests of the Tien Shan, the mighty Altai, the snowy peaks of the Alatau, the cliffs of Bayanaul with their innumerable mountain streams, their ravines and valleys clothed in luxuriant foliage and flowers, all leave an indelible impression. 'The country of birds without fear' is how a writer described Tengiz, the only fresh-water lake in the Markakol sanctuary. There are hundreds of shallow lakes scattered over the saline steppe—a bountiful region for migratory birds. The origin of Lake Shaytankol (in translation, 'Devil's lake') remains a mystery to this day, situated, as it is, on top of one of the Karkaralin Mountains, where there is also a ravine with famous caves.

A feeling for the long and fascinating history of Kazakhstan can be gained by visiting the old towns of the south, lying amidst cotton fields and vineyards, with their world-famous monuments of medieval architecture, the ruins of ancient cities and numerous burial mounds.

The land of the nomads, ancient yet eternally young, beautiful and unrepeatable, with its distinctive culture and kindly, hospitable people, will very soon open up its tourist routes to all who wish to see it with their own eyes.

177. The rockets and sputniks that are launched into space are actually assembled at the Baykonur cosmodrome, which was formerly the main site of the Soviet space programme.

178. All the complex technical procedures at the cosmodrome are controlled automatically. Baykonur is considered one of the safest launching sites in the world.

179. Military uniforms and military bands have always had an attraction for the young.

180. The protection of children's health, threatened in some regions by environmental factors, is a major priority in social welfare policy.

181. Religion is regaining its former importance in the life of the people of Kazakhstan. This young man who has been to the mosque to receive instruction reflects the growing interest in religion among the young.

182. The central park in Almaty is a favourite place to relax for the inhabitants of the capital, who number about 1.2 million.

183. *A network of railway lines connects the expanses of Kazakhstan. Trains are the most common means of internal travel.*

184. *Newlyweds and their guests indulge in a roadside celebration. More than one in five marriages in the country are 'mixed'—between persons of different nationality.*

185-189. Over one hundred nationalities make up the population of Kazakhstan. Kazakhs are the most numerous, followed by Russians, and then Ukrainians, Tatars, Uzbeks, Belorussians, Uygurs, Koreans, Germans, and smaller ethnic groups from Central Asia, the Caucasus and other parts of the former Soviet Union.

190. *Kazakhs are renowned for their hospitality. In towns, they like to invite friends, and especially guests from abroad, to discuss the latest news.*

191. *Hospitality in the yurt in the age-old style. The host ladles out 'koumiss', mare's milk, a highly nutritious drink which is used for the treatment of respiratory and other illnesses.*

A HISTORY OF KAZAKHSTAN IN DATES

Stone Age	2500 to 18th c. BC
Bronze Age	17th to 7th c. BC
529 BC	Campaign of Darius against the Saks
circa 330 BC	Campaign of Alexander of Macedon in Central Asia and southern Kazakhstan
4th c. BC to 3rd c. AD	Empire of the Huns
3rd to 2nd c. BC	States of Usuns and Kangyus
3rd to 4th c.	Age of great migration of peoples
542	First mention of the term 'Turki' (in a Chinese chronicle)
552	Formation of the steppe Turkic Empire: the Turkic kaganate
603	Collapse of the Turkic kaganate into western and eastern parts
702	Formation of the Tyurgesh kaganate
705-812	Arab invasion
751	Arab victory over the Chinese near Talas
756	Fall of the Tyurgesh kaganate
766-940	Karluk state
9th to 11th c.	Oguz state
965	Destruction by the Oguz and Prince Svyatoslav of Kievan Rus of the Khazar Kaganate
907-1125	Karakhitai state
907-1212	Karakhanid state
Early 11th to 13th c.	Kypchak states
1212-1224	Conquest of Kazakhstan and Central Asia by Chingis (Genghiz) Khan
1219-1220	Siege and destruction of Otrar by Mongols
1245-1247	Travels of Plano Carpini through the territory of Kazakhstan to Mongolia
1253-1255	Travels of Wilhelm Rubruk through the territory of Kazakhstan to Mongolia
14th to 15th c.	Completion of the forming of the Kazakh national identity
1456-66	Formation of the Kazakh khanate
1499-1557	Muhammad Haydar Doglati, historian and author of *Tarihi-i-Rashidi*
1500-1508	Muhammad Shaibani conquers much of Central Asia
1510	Kasym Khan re-establishes control over Kazakh territory

192. An elderly Kazakh. Old people are treated with great respect in Kazakh families, who do their best to ensure their comfort and well-being.

257

1595	Arrival of the Russian envoy Velyamin Stepanov to Khan Tevvekel
End of 18th c.	Khan Tauke codifies the law in the *Jeti Jargy*
1681-1688	Devastating incursions by the Jungars into Kazakhstan
1710	Congress of the Kazakh hordes to organize the struggle with Jungar feudal lords; election of the knight Bogenbay as leader of the Kazakh forces
1716-1717	Tauke appeals to Russia for military aid against Jungaria
1718	Kazakh embassy to Tsar Peter I
1720-1730	Years of Great Disasters (*Aktaban Shchubyryndy*); acceptance of Russian rule by Abu'l Khayr of the Little Horde
1740s	Middle Horde joins the Russian Empire
1758	Fall of Jungaria
1773-1775	Peasant revolt under the leadership of Emelyan Pugachov
1783-1797	Rebellion of the Kazakhs of the Little Horde under Syrym Datov
1835-1865	Chokan Valikhanov
1836-1837	Uprising led by Isatay Taymanov
1837-1846	Uprising led by Kenisary Kasymov
1845	Russians gain control over the Great Horde and abolish the remaining power of the Kazakh khans
1855-1856	Rebellion of the Aral Kazakhs
1870	Troubles in Mangyshlak (Mangystau)
1916	Rebellion against tsarist rule in Kazakhstan led by Amangeldy Imanov (1873-1919)
1917	October Revolution
1920	Kirgiz Autonomous Soviet Socialist Republic established (renamed Kazakh in 1923)
1936	Autonomous Kazakh Republic becomes the Kazakh Soviet Socialist Republic, a full member of the Union
1941-45	Great Patriotic War against the Axis powers
1954	Beginning of the opening up of the virgin lands of Kazakhstan
1991	Collapse of the Union of Soviet Socialist Republics; independence of the Republic of Kazakhstan; election of the first President of the Republic
1993	Constitution of the Republic of Kazakhstan promulgated

REIGNS OF THE KAZAKH KHANS

Girey and Janibek	1468-70 or 1473-74
Burunduk	1480-1511
Kasym	1511-18
Mamash	1518
Tahir	1523-33
Buydash	1533-34
Hak-Nazar	1538-80
Shigay	1580-82
Tavvakul (Tevvekel)	1583-98
Ishim (Yesim)	1598-1613
Tursun	1613-1627
Ishim (second time)	1627-28
Jihangir (Jangir)	1629-52
Tauke	1680-1718
Abulambet	1734-71
Abylay	1771-81
Bali (Uali)	1781-1819
Abu'l Khayr	1718-48
Kuraly	1748-86
Eraly	1791-94
Yesim	1796-97
Aychuvak	1797-1805
Aryngazy	1816-27

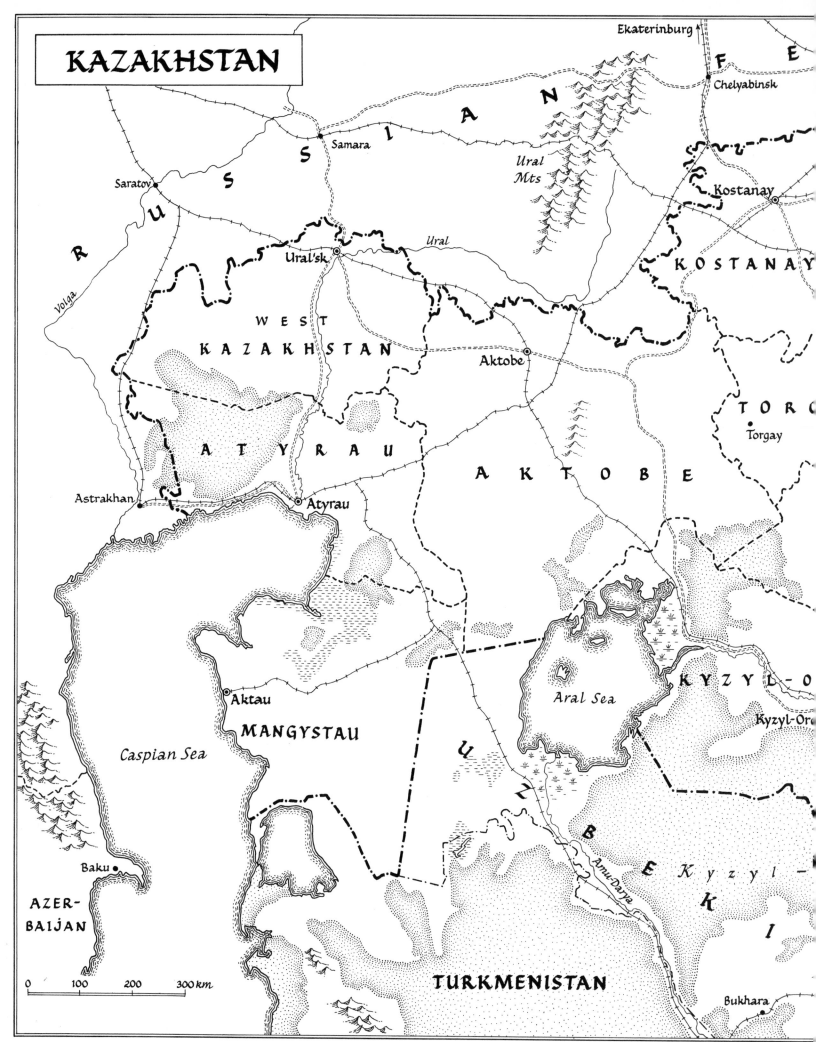

KAZAKHSTAN

Ekaterinburg

Chelyabinsk

Ural Mts

Kostanay

Samara

Saratov

K O S T A N A Y

Volga

Ural'sk

Ural

W E S T

K A Z A K H S T A N

Aktobe

A T Y R A U

A K T O B E

T O R G

Torgay

Astrakhan

Atyrau

K Y Z Y L - O

Aktau

Aral Sea

Kyzyl-Or

MANGYSTAU

Caspian Sea

U Z

B E K

Kyzyl-

Baku

Amu-Darya

AZER-
BAIJAN

0   100   200   300 km

TURKMENISTAN

Bukhara

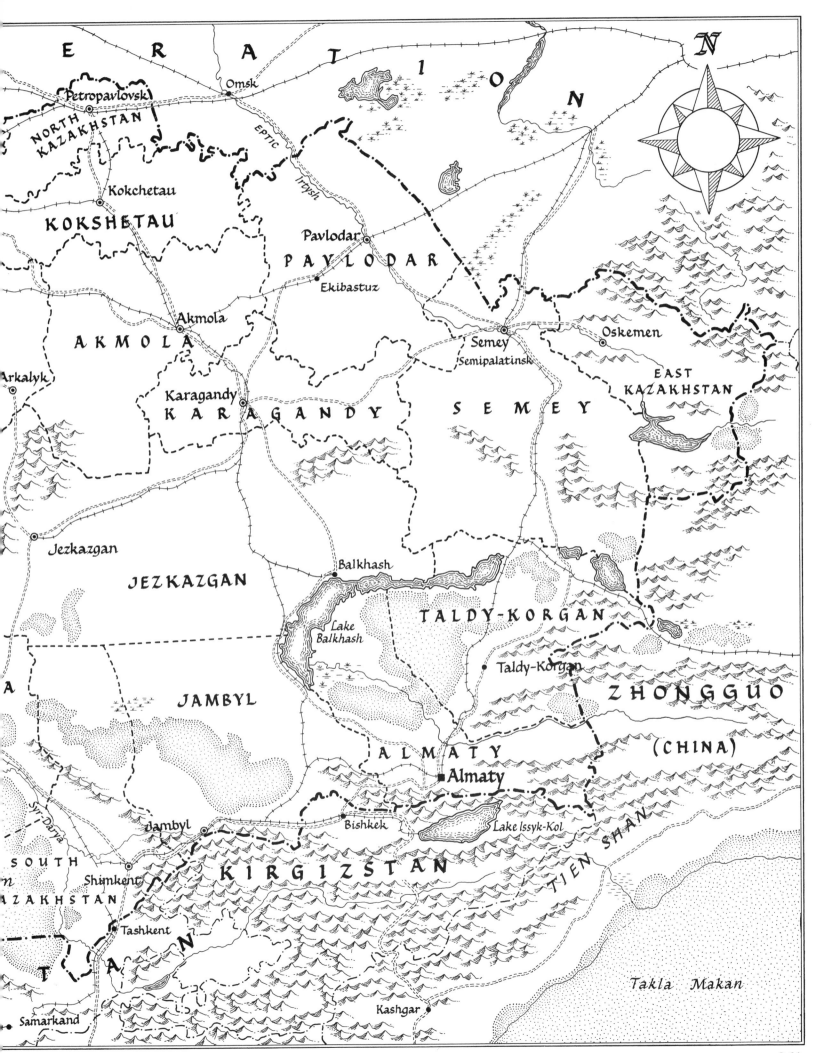

PROVINCES OF KAZAKHSTAN

Akmola

Area (sq. km.): 92,100
Population : 883,700
Persons per sq. km.: 9.6
Date of formation: 1939
Capital: Akmola
No. of inhabitants: 288,000
Distance from Almaty: 1,318 km.

This province, located in the north of the republic, was called Tselinograd from 1961, but renamed Akmola in 1992. It occupies the north-western part of the Sary Arka, on the upper course of the River Ishim. In the eastern and south-western parts rise the Ermentau and Jeldyadyr mountains.

The province has deposits of gold, bauxite, antimony, copper and hard coal.

The climate is extreme continental and drought-prone. The scorching summers bring dust storms and hot, dry winds. Winters are long, with little snow and strong winds.

The main river is the Ishim (a tributary of the Irtysh). The largest lakes are Tengiz, Korgaldpino and Kypshak. The major part of the territory lies in the steppe zone, much of it comprising saline soils and semi-desert.

The population of the province is made up of 193,700 Kazakhs (22%), 400,900 Russians (46%), 112,300 Germans (20.9%), 73,700 Ukrainians (8.5%), and smaller numbers of Belorussians, Tatars, Poles and Uzbeks. The most densely settled areas are the north and central parts, the valley of the Ishim. Besides the capital, Akmola, the main towns are Atbasar, Alekseevka, Ermentau and Makinsk.

As a result of the opening up of the virgin lands in the province, grain growing became highly developed: cereals account for 51% of its agricultural produce. In the years 1954-58, four million hectares of grasslands were ploughed up. The main branches of farming are arable, and the breeding of livestock for meat and sheep for wool. Non-ferrous metal ores are mined and engineering and metal working are developed.

There are plans to move the capital of Kazakhstan to the city of Akmola.

Aktobe

Area (sq. km.): 298,700
Population: 758,400
Persons per sq. km: 2.5
Date of formation: 1932
Capital: Aktobe
No. of inhabitants: 267,600
Distance from Almaty: 2,280 km.

This province in the north-western part of the republic is divided into 16 administrative regions, and has six cities and three smaller urban settlements. The capital of the same name, founded in 1869, is located on the banks of the River Elek.

Aktobe province is mostly tableland with characteristic alternations of broad plateaus and lower areas. In the northern part are the foothills of the Ural Mountains, and in the central part the Mugodjar Mountains, which reach a height of 657 m. In the south-east extend massifs of sand hillocks—the Aral Karakum, Big and Small Barsuk deserts, and in the north-east, the Torgay plateau, intersected by ravines. In the east the land descends to the Torgay depression, while in the south it rises to the Ustyurt plateau. On the Ustyurt plateau, between the Caspian and Aral seas, giant furrows of unknown origin and purpose have been discovered. This remarkable archaeological find, on a grander scale than the mysterious furrows of Nasca in Peru, are of immense scientific interest and significance.

The climate is extreme continental: the temperature in winter can fall to 48°C below zero, and in summer rises to 43° C. Spring and autumn are short, with an abrupt transition from the cold winter to the hot summer. Strong winds are frequent in autumn, blizzards in winter, and dust storms in summer. Drought is not uncommon.

The main rivers are the Shel, Or, Elek, Torgay, Irgiz, Oyil and Sagyz. Many rivers dry up in summer or diminish considerably. There are 150 small lakes, many of them salty.

The population comprises 407,200 Kazakhs, who make up 55.6% of the total population, 173,300 Germans, 16,900 Tatars and smaller numbers of Belorussians, Moldavians,

Chechens, Bashkirs, Azerbaijanis (Azeri), Bolgars, Koreans and Mordvins.

The mixed economy is based on metallurgy, the chemical industry, engineering, livestock farming and the cultivation of cereals. All the extraction of chrome-nickel ore and all the production of chrome salts and x-ray apparatus are concentrated in Aktobe.

Almaty

Area (sq. km.): 104,900
Population: 965,800 (excluding capital)
Persons per sq. km.: 9.2
Date of formation: 1932
Capital: Almaty
No. of inhabitants: 1,182,100

This province in the south-east of the country has 11 administrative regions, four cities and six smaller urban settlements.

The north-western part is a gently sloping plain which extends to Lake Balkhash. Most of the territory is covered by the sandy hills of the Saryesik Altau, Taukum and Korgankum. In the south-east rise mighty mountain ranges, covered with eternal snow and ice, that are part of the Tien Shan system, with the highest peak in Kazakhstan, Khan-Tengri (6,995 m.). Almaty is located by the foothills of the northern Tien Shan and the Zaili Alatau (i.e. the Altau beyond the River Ili), which in the east divides into three spurs. The southern slopes of the Zaili Alatau descend steeply to the valleys of the rivers Chilik and Chonkemin. The Zaili Alatau, intersected by deep ravines and canyons, are prone to floods and avalanches and have large areas of permafrost.

The foothills of the mountains are rich in mineral resources. Building materials, brown coal and mixed metallic ores are extracted in the province.

In the lowland part of the province, the climate is extreme continental: the mean temperature in January is 14°C below zero, and in July 24°C. In the foothills, the climate is milder but more unpredictable.

In the delta of the Ili, the biggest river in the province, lies the Bakanas plain, crisscrossed by dry river beds and old water courses. The province has a number of freshwater and salt-water lakes, the biggest of which is Balkhash, which has a maximum depth of 26 m. and is partly saline and partly freshwater. In the foothills of the Zaili Alatau there are many mineral springs.

Kapchagay, the second largest artificial lake in the country (after Bukhtamir), with an area of 1,850 sq. km., and the Kapchagay hydro-electric power station have been constructed on the Ili. Kapchagay is of great importance for both energy production and irrigation. It is also a delightful recreation place for the citizens of Almaty.

The shores of Lake Balkhash are marshy, with dense thickets of reeds and willows. In the lowlands there are sandy hills, saline areas and infertile terrain with poor grassy vegetation. At a height of 600 m. the semi-desert gives way to a zone of dry feather-grass steppe. From 800 to 1,700 m. there are meadows, deciduous woods, and apple, apricot, plum and other fruit trees. Above 1,500 m. begin sub-alpine meadows in combination with coniferous forests, and above 2,000 m. the alpine meadows.

In the mountains the wildlife includes snow leopard, lynx, wild sheep, brown bear, mountain goat, Siberian deer and various fur-bearing animals. The lower areas of the province have a variety of snakes, tortoises, lizards and poisonous insects.

The population is made up of 406,800 Kazakhs, 294,200 Russians, 103,700 Uygurs, 61,300 Germans, 19,100 Turks, 18,500 Ukrainians and many other nationalities. Apart from Almaty, the towns of some size are Kaskelen, Talgar and Issyk.

The most important industrial activities are engineering, metal-working, light industry, food processing, logging and wood-working. The main branches of agriculture are farming (with irrigation) and pastoral livestock breeding.

Almaty, the capital of both the province and the republic, is at the hub of a network of air and rail communications. The gas pipeline from Bukhara to Almaty is of vital importance to the economy of the province. The city has 213 km. of tram lines and 92 km. of trolleybus lines.

Atyrau

Area (sq. km.): 113,500
Population: 449,100
Persons per sq. km.: 4
Date of formation: 1938
Capital: Atyrau
No. of inhabitants: 152,800
Distance from Almaty: 2,664 km.

This province lies in the west of Kazakhstan, north of the Caspian Sea. Its western frontier is demarcated by the Volga, which forms the border with the Astrakhan province of Russia. It is divided into eight rural districts, and has one city and 16 smaller urban settlements. The provincial capital, Atyrau, on the River Ural, was founded in 1640.

Atyrau occupies much of the Caspian lowlands, which in the south-east extend to the northern edge of the Ustyurt plateau, rising to an altitude of 300 m. A significant part of the lowlands is arid and cannot support vegetation. Large deposits of oil and gas have been discovered here.

The climate is extremely dry, with hot summers and cold winters. The temperature in January ranges between 3° and 10°C below zero, and in July averages 26°C. Hot, dry winds and dust storms are quite common.

The main rivers are the Ural, Emba, Sagyz, Shel and Oyil. In summer the rivers shrink and sometimes disappear. The lakes, of which Inder is the largest, are mainly saline and dry up partially or completely in summer, forming salt marshes.

The vegetation is characteristic of semi-desert and desert zones. Much of the province is covered by wormwood scrub, but on the shores of the Caspian Sea and in the valleys of the rivers Ural, Emba and Sagyz there are grasses. Groves of poplar and willow edge the rivers. Wildlife is represented by birds of prey, rodents and hoofed animals. In the waters of the Caspian and the River Ural, white sturgeon, stellate sturgeon, pike-perch, carp and bream are to be found.

About 61% of the province's inhabitants live in urban areas and 39% in villages. The most densely populated areas are along the River Ural and the left branches of the Volga delta. The Kazakhs make up 79.8% of the population, Russians 15%. There are also Ukrainians, Tatars, Koreans, Germans and Belorussians.

The basis of the province's economy is oil production, fishing and livestock farming. The oil refining and petro-chemical industries and fish processing are already well developed, while engineering, metal-working, and the manufacture and repair of equipment for the oil and fishing industries are all expanding.

The raising of livestock is the most important branch of farming. In the flood valley of the Ural, cereals, melons and water melons are grown.

Atyrau province has 749 km. of railways and 3,000 km. of roads.

East Kazakhstan

Area (sq. km.): 97,300
Population: 960,300
Persons per sq. km.: 9.9
Date of formation: 1932
Capital: Ust-Kamenogorsk
No. of inhabitants: 335,100
Distance from Almaty: 1,316 km.

The province has 12 regions, six cities and 17 smaller urban settlements. Its capital, Ust-Kamenogorsk, was founded in 1720.

Its territory is mostly mountainous, and includes the peaks of the Rudnoy Altai and the South Altai. The valley of the River Irtysh is the main lowland area.

East Kazakhstan is rich in minerals, especially metallic ores: lead, zinc, copper, gold, silver and rare metals—cadmium, molybdenum, bismuth, indium and thallium. There are also deposits of coal, oil shale and marble.

The climate is extreme continental. The mean winter temperature in the plains and foothills is around 18°C below zero, and in the mountains the absolute minimum is minus 55°C. The summer is moderately hot: in July the temperature averages 23°C, but can rise as high as 41°C. Precipitation is variable.

The main river is the Irtysh. The biggest lakes are Zaysan, Markakol and three large artificial lakes.

Vegetation depends on altitude: in the lower areas there is feather grass, in the middle zone woodland predominates, and between 2,000 and 3,000 m. is a zone of alpine and sub-alpine meadows. The province's fauna includes elk, wild goat, Siberian deer, brown bear, lynx, snow leopard, wolf and wild boar. Fox and mink are farmed for their fur. Swans, cormorants and cranes feature among the birds. The waters are abundant in fish.

The population, 65% urban, is made up of 253,700 Kazakhs, 613,800 Russians, 22,800 Germans, 16,200 Ukrainians, and also Tatars, Belorussians and Uzbeks.

Livestock raising is the main branch of farming. Siberian and other deer are bred, and in the foothills of the Altai bees are kept. The main industrial branches are non-ferrous metallurgy, engineering, and wood-working. The main power plants are the Bukhtarlinsk and Ust-Kamenogorsk hydro-electric stations and the Leninogorsk coal-fired station.

The railways, which have a total length of 426 km., play an important role in transporting goods. The main railway junction is Oskemen. Goods are also carried by water along the Irtysh and the Bukhtarlinsk artificial lake. The road network totals 4,300 km.

194-196. Camels are raised in almost all regions of Kazakhstan. Camel's milk, 'shubat', is highly valued and is used as a medicinal drink in many medical institutions. Camel-hair is also another valued product.

197. The two-humped camel, being more resistant to cold, is mainly bred in the north-western provinces of Kazakhstan, while the dromedary is found mostly in the south (overleaf).

198. A view of a modern Kazakh aul in winter. (pp. 270-1)

199, 200. The number of private farms in the republic has reached 9,000. A national development programme makes provision for the revival of the agro-industrial sector. Meanwhile the farmers must get by on their own resources.

201-204. The horse has always played a vital role in the life of the rural population and is still essential for getting about in remote areas. Horse meat and mare's milk feature prominently in the traditional Kazakh diet. Depending on the season and the quality of pasturage, mare's milk is classified as summer, autumn and winter 'koumiss', which differ significantly in taste. There are some one and a half million horses in the country.

205. Life in isolated farming communities is hard, especially in winter. All members of the family, even children, have their own duties, and all must pull their weight.

206. Farming families, lacking outside distractions, are particularly close-knit. If need be, husband and wife will set off on horseback together to get supplies or visit neighbours.

*207. A son shakes hands with his
relations as he leaves for distant parts.*

208. Grain growing is more developed in the northern regions, while in the south, cotton is the most important crop. The Pakhtaral State Farm, pictured here, is the biggest cotton producer in the country.

Jambyl

Area (sq. km.): 144,200
Population: 1,059,000
Persons per sq. km.: 7.3
Date of formation: 1939
Capital: Jambyl
No. of inhabitants: 315,100
Distance from Almaty: 554 km.

This southern province is divided into 10 administrative regions, and has three cities, apart from Jambyl, and 13 smaller urban settlements. The provincial capital, Jambyl, grew up on the site of the ancient town of Taraz.

Its territory, mostly comprising plains, is bisected by the River Chu. The northern part is made up of the clayey desert of Moyunkum with undulating dunes. In the south-east is the Karatau range, and in the south, the Kirgiz Alatau. In the south-east the Jalatau, Artau and Kindykta join up with the Zaili Alatau.

Deposits of phosphorites, non-ferrous metals and hard coal are mined.

The climate is mostly extreme continental, although somewhat milder in the foothills.

The rivers of the province flow into the Aral Sea and Lake Balkhash. The biggest are the Chu and the Talas. The western part of Lake Balkhash is located in Jambyl province, as are lakes Bilikol, Aktol and Ashchikol, all abundant in fish, and two big artificial lakes: Tasutkol and Akkol.

The steppe-desert belt below the mountains is barren and saline, with saxaul growing in the sands. In the river valleys there are willow groves, reed marshes, thickets of tamarisk, occasional woods of aspen and maple, and on the stony slopes, tree-like bushes of araka. Many rodents and poisonous insects and reptiles live in the sands, such as the falanga and karakurt spiders, scorpions, tarantulas and snakes. In the river valleys there are wild cat, pheasant and musk-rat.

The population of the province consists of Kazakhs (48.8%), Russians (26.5%), and also Germans, Ukrainians, Tatars, Turks, Uygurs, Kirgiz, Belorussians, Chechens and Bashkirs. The most densely populated areas are the foothills of the Kirgiz Alatau, the valley of the Chu, and the valleys in the Karatau range.

The economy is based on industry combined with developed irrigated farming and livestock breeding. The chemical, light manufacturing and food-processing industries, which draw on locally available raw materials, are the main industrial branches. Jambyl occupies first place in Kazakhstan in the manufacture of leather footwear.

In the foothills, fine-fleeced and other varieties of sheep are raised, and in the northern desert regions, astrakhan sheep. Crops include wheat, sweet corn, barley, millet, vegetables, melons and watermelons.

Jezkazgan

Area (sq. km.): 313,400
Population: 496,500
Persons per sq. km.: 1.6
Date of formation: 1973
Capital: Jezkazgan
No. of inhabitants: 111,700
Distance from Almaty: 1,367 km.

This central province has seven regions, three cities, and 22 smaller urban settlements. The capital, Jezkazgan, was founded in 1954.

The northern part is covered by the low Sary Arka hills. In the east lie the Kyzylaray and Kyzyltas mountains, and in the west, the Ulytau mountains. The territory in the south-west is covered by sandy tableland: the Aral Karakum, Mynbulak, Aryskum and Moyunkum deserts, and in the south includes the edge of the Betpak-Dalasalt desert.

There is very little surface water: the majority of the small rivers are shallow and saline, and many rivers have dried up completely.

In the mountains, there are pine, birch and aspen forests, and alongside the rivers various types of willow and broom. Woodland occupies an area of 29,000 hectares. The varied wildlife includes gazelle, wild sheep, wild goat, steppe antelope, willow grouse and black grouse.

The population is made up of Kazakhs (46%), Russians (34.9%), Germans (4.9%) and people of a dozen other nationalities.

The most developed branches of the economy are mining, non-ferrous metallurgy and the light manufacturing and food industries. The main rural occupation is livestock farming: sheep rearing, horse and camel breeding and poultry farming. Arable farming occupies a secondary place, but cereals and fodder crops are grown.

Jezkazgan has 1,248 km. of railways and 4,000 km. of paved roads.

209. The horse is the Kazakh's faithful companion, his pride and joy.

281

Karagandy

Area (sq. km.): 117,900
Population: 1,343,300
Persons per sq. km.: 11.4
Date of formation: 1932
Capital: Karagandy
No. of inhabitants: 607,200
Distance from Almaty: 1,096 km.

This central province is divided into nine administrative regions, and has six cities and 15 smaller urban settlements.

Most of the province is covered by the low Sary Arka hills, the vestiges of a once mighty mountain system, and undulating tableland. In the south-eastern part the low hills ascend to the scenic Karkaralin massifs, intersected by gorges and river valleys.

The province is rich in minerals and raw materials, especially hard coal. The Karagandy basin contains 30% of the republic's known reserves of hard coal and 100% of coking coal. In the eastern part there are iron ore deposits.

The climate is extreme continental. The mean temperature in January is 19°C below zero, and in July 21°C.

The biggest river is the Nura, on which the Samarkand reservoir has been created. In summer, many streams dry up. The Irtysh-Karagandy Canal, which is of immense importance to the economy of the province, is 500 km. long and has 20 stations, which raise the water level by 420 m. The canal also provides water for the farmlands of neighbouring Pavlodar and Akmola provinces.

The river and mountain valleys have lush grass and meadow plants. In the mountains of Karkarala, pine and birch woods cover 88,500 hectares. The fauna here includes mountain sheep, hornless deer, wolf and fox.

The population, 85% urban, is made up of 231,800 Kazakhs (17.2%), 703,600 Russians (52.2%), 143,500 Germans (10.7%), 107,100 Ukrainians, 45,800 Tatars, and smaller numbers of Lithuanians, Armenians, Jews, Bolgars, Udmurts, Mari, Turkmen, Georgians, Moldovians, Azerbaijanis (Azeri), Chuvash, Greeks and many others. The central part of the province is the most densely settled.

Coal provides the basis for the province's industry. The town of Temirtau, which has grown up around a large metallurgical complex, specializes in ferrous metallurgy. Engineering works turn out equipment for heavy industry. Electric power production is based on local coal.

There are 112 state farms, mostly engaged in grain growing and sheep and horse breeding.

The railway network of 581 km. is of prime importance in linking the province to the main industrial centres of Kazakhstan. Within the province, most of the transport is by road. The Pavlodar-Karagandy-Shimkent oil pipeline crosses Karagandy.

Kokshetau

Area (sq. km.): 78,100
Population: 675,800
Persons per sq. km.: 8.7
Date of formation: 1944
Capital: Kokshetau
No. of inhabitants: 145,200
Distance from Almaty: 1,615 km.

This northern province borders on the Akmola, Torgay, Kostanay and Pavlodar provinces, and in the north-east on the Omsk province of Russia. It is divided into 16 administrative regions, and has four cities and eight smaller urban settlements.

The territory of the province is mostly high tableland. The north-eastern part is the southern edge of the Western Siberian plain and in the south-west it joins the northern edge of the Sary Arka. The most beautiful region is the Kokshetau Mountains, where Mount Kokshe is the highest point (947m.). The province is noted as a resort area, with many sanatoria and rest houses in the pine and birch forests of Kokshetau.

The depostits of hard coal, dolomite, gold, limestone and common salt are exploited.

The climate is mostly continental, though less extreme in the mountain areas.

The province has abundant surface water. The main rivers are the Ishim in the west, the Chinginka crossing the central part, and the Selety in the east. There are also many freshwater and salt-water lakes, and underground water is widely used.

The population comprises 191,300 Kazakhs (28.9%), 261,800 Russians (39.5%), 82,000 Germans (12.4%), 55,600 Ukrainians (8.4%), 25,400 Poles, and other nationalities. Besides Kokshetau, the towns are Krasnoarmeisk, Shuchinsk and Stepnyak.

Grain growing plays a significant role in the economy. The province has 6.6 million hectares of agricultural land, of which 3,606,100 hectares are cultivated; 80% of this is sown with grain crops. Livestock farming concentrates on the raising of fine-fleeced sheep. The food-processing and instrument manufacturing industry are well developed.

Starting from the basis of a small cast-iron foundry and machine tool factories which were evacuated to the province during the Second World War, an important plant has grown up which manufactures and exports automatic and semi-automatic weighing machines. Also of republican importance is the factory for breathing apparatus.

The railway network, 1,100 km. in length, is connected to the Urals, Siberia and the central and southern economic regions. There are 7,700 km. of roads in Kokshetau.

Kostanay

Area (sq. km.): 114,500
Population: 1,086,500
Persons per sq. km.: 9.5
Date of formation: 1936
Capital: Kostanay
No. of inhabitants: 237,100
Distance from Almaty: 2,419 km.

This northern part of the republic borders on the Korgansk, Chelyabinsk and Orenburg provinces of the Russian Federation, and on the Aktobe, Torgay and Kokshetau provinces of Kazakhstan. It is divided into 13 administrative regions, and has four cities and 13 smaller urban settlements. Its capital, Kostanay, on the River Tobol, was founded in 1883.

The province is located in the region where the Ural Mountains, the Western Siberian plain and the Torgay plateau converge. Much of its territory is hilly tableland, with the highest point, Jetygara (412 m.), in the west. Kostanay is rich in industrial raw materials: magnetite and iron ores, bauxite, brown coal, asbestos, brick clays and building stone.

The climate is moderate continental, with cold winters and fairly warm summers.

The main rivers are the Tobol and its tributaries. There are many large and small lakes, the majority freshwater.

In the northern and central parts the surface cover is mainly grass. Pine woods grow in sandy areas. The fauna is similar to that of the other northern provinces.

The population, 54% urban, comprises 183,600 Kazakhs (17.5%), 494,200 Russians (47%), 166,000 Ukrainians (15.8%), 107,400 Germans (10.2%) and many other nationalities. The northern part of the province is the most densely settled. Besides the capital, the towns are Jetygara, Rudny and Lisakovsky.

As regards natural resources and economic specialization, the province divides into northern and southern regions. The northern wooded steppe and steppe zone is rich in iron ore and asbestos. The metal-working, electric power and building materials industries are concentrated here, and there is also mixed farming. The main sectors of the southern economy are grain growing and livestock breeding. By the opening up of the virgin lands, Kostanay has become the granary of the republic, with 5,872,400 hectares under crops.

The railway network is 1,137 km. in length, and there are 5,700 km. of roads.

Kyzyl-Orda

Area (sq. km.): 228,100
Population: 591,200
Persons per sq. km.: 2.6
Date of formation: 1938
Capital: Kyzyl-Orda
No. of inhabitants: 162,100
Distance from Almaty: 1,227 km.

One of the southern provinces of the republic, Kyzyl-Orda borders on the Jezkazgan, Aktobe and South Kazakhstan provinces and on Uzbekistan. It is divided into eight regions, and has three cities and nine smaller urban settlements. The capital, Kyzyl-Orda, is one of the oldest cities of the Jeti Su (Seven Rivers) region. Before 1853 it was called Ak-Mechet, and until 1925, Perovsk.

The greater part of the province is located in the desert zone of the Turanian lowlands. It includes the lower part of the Syr Darya and considerable areas of the northern and eastern shores of the Aral Sea, as well as the islands in it. In the eastern part are the slopes of the Karatau Mountains, in the south, the sands of the Kyzylkum (Red Desert), and in the north-western part the dunes of the Aral Karakum. On the shores of the Aral Sea and other shallow lakes, there are layers of saline therapeutic muds and quartz sands.

This is one of the most drought-stricken and hottest regions of Kazakhstan. Hot, dry winds blow in the summer, when the temperature sometimes reaches 46°C. The scant precipitation is mostly in spring and autumn. The winter is warm with little snow.

The Syr Darya, which flows through the central part of the province from the south-east to the north-west for over 1,000 km., forms many branches with marshy water courses. The fertile soil and water meadows of the Syr Darya valley are the mainstay of the economy of this region. With its abundant water and long warm summers, the valley is ideal for growing rice, grapes, melons and watermelons. In the desert regions huge subterranean reserves of fresh water have been found.

The fauna is of the desert and semi-desert type. A state nature reserve was founded on the island of Barsakelmes with the aim of preserving and breeding many species of wildlife. As the ecological situation in the Aral Sea area has deteriorated, the animals have been transferred to other wildlife sanctuaries.

The population is mainly made up of Kazakhs (79.4%) and Russians (13.3%), with smaller numbers of Koreans, Ukrainians, Germans, Tatars, Belorussians, Uzbeks and Chechens. Besides Kyzyl-Orda, the towns are Aralsk and Kazalin.

The province specializes in the food-processing and salt-extraction industries, irrigated farming, the raising of karakul and fine-fleeced sheep and camel breeding. The building materials industry is being developed on the basis of the plentiful raw material resources. Kyzyl-Orda has one of the largest fish processing factories and produces cooking salt and refined rice. The juicy and fragrant Torlama melon is grown here.

The Baykonur cosmodrome is located on the territory of the province.

Mangystau

Area (sq. km.):165,100
Population: 345,200
Persons per sq. km.: 2.1
Date of formation: 1973
Capital: Aktau
No. of inhabitants: 177,200
Distance from Almaty: 3,267 km.

Situated in the south-west of the country, it was formed in 1973 as the Mangyshlak province, but in 1990 it was renamed Mangystau. It has borders with the Aktobe and Atyrau provinces of Kazakhstan, in the east with the Karakalpak Republic, and in the south with the Republic of Turkmenistan. In the west it is edged by the Caspian Sea. It is divided into three administrative regions, and has three cities and 13 smaller urban settlements. The capital, Aktau, a port on the Caspian Sea, was founded as a completely new town in 1963. In 1978 the International Union of Architects awarded a group of architects and constructors of the town a gold medal and the Patrick Abercrombie Prize for creating a town with ample greenery and water in difficult natural conditions.

The province is situated in the Caspian lowlands and the western part of the Ustyurt plateau. Its relief is remarkably varied, ranging from low hills and mountains of medium height to undulating plains, broad depressions and sand dunes. The Mangystau Mountains rise in the central part, and the Karatau and Aktau highlands extend from the north-west to the south-east. The northern and southern parts are plains. In the south, along the shores of the Caspian Sea is the Karaky depression, the lowest area of land in Eurasia.

Large reserves of oil and gas have been found in the province, and also deposits of phosphorites, coal, manganese, various salts and building stone.

The climate is extreme continental and very dry. There is little surface water, and a significant part of the territory is made up of saline soil and barren salty areas. Small rivers and streams appear in the spring, when the desert becomes green for a short period of time.

The fauna includes hoofed animals, predators, rodents and birds. In addition to abundant fish, seals can be found in the Caspian Sea.

The population, 88% urban, comprises 165,000 Kazakhs (50.9%), 106,800 Russians (32.9%), and also Ukrainians, Lezgins, Azerbaijanis (Azeri) Armenians, Chechens, Belorussians, Ingush, Germans and Ossetians. It is concentrated in the oil industry regions and on the shores of the Caspian Sea.

The economy of the province began to develop intensively from 1960 with the opening up of the oil and gas fields. Almost 85% of the extraction of oil and 90% of natural gas is concentrated in the Mangystau fuel-oil industrial complex. The towns of Uzen, Jetybay, Tasbulat, Tenge and Buzachi are based on the oil and gas fields. Electricity is produced by oil-powered stations, and atomic energy is also used. (The town of Aktau has a fast neutron atomic reactor). Floating fish factories operate in the Caspian Sea, and large fish-processing plants are located in the towns of Fort Shevchenko and Bautino.

The natural conditions are not suitable for arable farming, but sheep, horses and camels are raised.

Railways, pipelines and water transport are all important for the economy. The port towns are Bautino, Aktau and Eraliev.

North Kazakhstan

Area (sq. km.): 44,300
Population: 617,500
Persons per sq. km.: 13.9
Date of formation: 1936
Capital: Petropavlovsk
No. of inhabitants: 248,700
Distance from Almaty: 1,809 km.

This northern province borders on the Korgansk, Tyumen and Omsk province of the Russian Federation, and in the south on the Kokshetau and Kostanay provinces. It is divided into 12 administrative regions, and has four cities and one smaller urban settlement. Over 40% of the province's population live in the capital, Petropavlovsk, founded in 1752, which lies on the River Ishim.

The relief of the province is characterized by many depressions around the lakes, expanses of steppe, and high mountains. Building stone, gravel and clay are extracted.

The climate is continental: the winters are long and severe and the summers hot. The mean temperature in January is 19°C below zero, and in July, 19.5°C.

The Sergeev artificial lake has been created on the River Ishim, which flows for 400 km. through the province. There are more than 1,000 shallow lakes, mostly freshwater.

Much of North Kazakhstan is wooded-steppe zone, in which birch predominates. The wildlife includes elk, wild goat, ermine, weasel and a variety of birds.

The province is inhabited by 111,600 Kazakhs (18.6%), 372,300 Russians (62.1%), 39,300 Germans (6.6%), 38,000 Ukrainians (6.3%), and also Tatars, Poles, Chuvash, Bashkirs and Azerbaijanis (Azeri). The urban population forms just under half the total. Besides Petropavlovsk, the main towns are Bulaevo, Mamlyutka and Sergeevka.

The economy is of mixed type. Engineering is a major branch of industry, with factories manufacturing motors and agricultural machinery. The flour-milling, meat-processing and dairy industries are also of importance. North Kazakhstan is one of the country's leading grain producing areas, cultivating spring wheat, barley, oats and buckwheat, as well as legumes and olives. The raising of livestock for meat is also well developed.

There are 371 km. of railways and 4,000 km. of roads in the province.

Pavlodar

Area (sq. km.): 127,500
Population: 971,700
Persons per sq. km.: 7.6
Date of formation: 1938
Capital: Pavlodar
No. of inhabitants: 352,900
Distance from Almaty: 1,758 km.

This province in the north-east of the republic, on the middle course of the Irtysh, borders in the north on the Omsk and Novosibirsk provinces and the Altai region of the Russian Federation, and on the Semipalatinsk (Semey), Karagandy, Akmola and Kokshetau provinces of Kazakhstan. It is divided into 12 administrative regions, and has four cities, and 11 smaller urban settlements. The capital of the province, Pavlodar, founded in 1861, lies on the River Irtysh and has 30% of the province's population.

The territory of the province falls within the steppe and semi-desert zones. Its highest point is Mount Aulie (1,055 m.). Pavlodar has rich deposits of hard coal, brown coal, copper and mixed metallic ores, and salt.

The climate is extreme continental, with long, severe winters and hot, dry summers. The main river, the Irtysh, flows for 500 km. through the province. The smaller rivers mostly dry up in the summer. There are many lakes, the majority saline.

The vegetation and fauna are typical of the steppe regions. In the north-west extensive forests of pine and birch have been preserved.

The population comprises 268,500 Kazakhs (28.5%), 427,700 Russians (45.4%), 95,300 Germans (10.1%), 86,700 Ukrainians (9.2%), and many other nationalities. Besides the capital, the main towns are Ekibastuz, Ermak and Irtysh.

The economy is based on mining, energy production, and the metallurgical, engineering and chemical industries. The mainstays of the economy are the Bogatyr open-cast coal mine—one of the most important in the world, the thermal-electric power stations in Ekibastuz, the tractor factory, aluminium works and oil refinery in Pavlodar, and the ferro-alloy plant and very large hydro-electric power station in the town of Ermak.

Agriculture was intensively developed with the opening up of the virgin lands. The northern part of the province, which has 70% of the cultivated land, is the main region for grain growing. Fine-fleeced sheep are the most common livestock. In the semi-desert and Sary Arka regions, hunting is practised. Timber is felled in the forests along the Irtysh.

The province has 733 km. of railways and 5,000 km. of roads.

Semipalatinsk (Semey)

Area (sq. km.): 179,600
Population: 846,600
Persons per sq. km.: 4.7
Date of formation: 1939
Capital: Semipalatinsk (Semey)
No. of inhabitants: 345,200
Distance from Almaty: 1,016 km.

This eastern province, borders on the Altai region of the Russian Federation and the Pavlodar, East Kazakhstan, Karagandy and Taldy-Korgan provinces. It is divided into 13 administrative regions, and has two cities and 12 smaller urban settlements. The capital, Semipalatinsk (Kazakh: Semey), was founded in 1782.

The province lies mainly in the steppe and semi-desert zones. All the western and central part is covered by the low Sary Arka hills. In the north-west and south-east the Chingistan and Akshatau ranges extend to the western edges of the Tarbagatay. The highest peak is Tastau (2,992 m). The eastern part of the Sary Arka is bordered by the massifs of the Kolbin range and by the Zaysan basin. Deposits of non-ferrous and rare metals, graphite, Glauber's and common salt, and manganese are exploited.

The climate is extreme continental, with a particularly wide range of temperature in the south-east: during the long winter it can reach minus 51°C, and in summer, 43°C. There are frequent blizzards in winter and dust storms in summer.

The main river is the Irtysh. Several big lakes—Zaysan, Sasykkol, Alakol—lie partly within the territory of the province.

The population consists of 432,800 Kazakhs (51.9%), 300,500 Russians (36.0%), 44,100 Germans (5.3%), and smaller numbers of Tatars, Belorussians, Chechens and Uzbeks. Besides the capital, the main towns are Ayaguz and Chara.

The province is the most important for livestock raising in the republic. The meat-processing complex of Semipalatinsk was among the biggest in the Soviet Union. On the southern slopes of the Tarbagatay there are orchards and vineyards, and crop farming is carried on with the use of irrigation. In addition, engineering, metal-working, ship building and repair, and the production of cement and reinforced concrete are developed.

The Semipalatinsk nuclear testing ground is located in the steppe near the mountainous region of Degelen.

The province has 755 km. of railways and 5,500 km. of roads.

South Kazakhstan

Area (sq. km.): 16,300
Population: 1,912,400
Persons per sq. km.: 16.4
Date of formation: 1932
Capital: Shimkent
No. of inhabitants: 402,700
Distance from Almaty: 775 km.

Lying in the south of the republic, in the Syr Darya river basin, the province is mainly lowlying plain, with the Betpak-Dala salt basin (500 km. in length) in the north. To the south of the valley of the River Chu lies the Moyunkum Desert, to the west, the sandy desert of Kyzylkum and the steppes of Chardara, and in the far south, the Myrzashol Desert. The Karatau range crosses the centre of the province.

South Kazakhstan has important reserves of iron ore, mixed metallic ores, brown coal, marble, and other minerals.

The climate is continental: the mean temperature in January is minus 9°C, and in July, 29°C.

The major river is the Syr Darya, which has many tributaries. There are four big lakes and the large Burgund and Chardara reservoirs, created on dry river beds.

Vegetation is varied: in the sands, saxaul and prickly bushes grow; in the river valleys, groves of willow; in the forests, there are fruit and nut trees; the higher slopes of the mountains have sub-alpine and alpine pastures. The sandy deserts are the habitat of many lizards and snakes, steppe tortoises, rodents, and hoofed animals such as the steppe antelope and gazelle. In the valleys of the Chu and Syr Darya, there are wild boar, reed cats and many water birds. Wild sheep, mountain goat and bear live in the mountain forests, and the snow leopard is found in the high mountains. In the Talas Alatau, the Aksu Jabaglinsky Sanctuary has been established.

The population is made up of 1,012,300 Kazakhs (55.7%), 285,000 Uzbeks (15.7%), 278,500 Russians (15.3%), 44,500 Germans (2.4%), and also Tatars, Koreans, Turks, Chechens, Belorussians, Tadzhiks, Greeks, Jews, Mordvins, Armenians, Kirgiz and Persians.

South Kazakhstan is one of the main cotton growing regions of the republic. One of its centres is the large Pakhtaral state farm. Cereals, melons, water melons and other fruit are major crops in this region, which is famous for its orchards and vineyards. Astrakhan and fine-fleeced sheep are bred.

Electricity production is based on water power, natural gas and transported coal. In the mountainous Karatau region, various metallic ores are extracted, providing the raw materials for the lead-zinc refinery in the capital, Shimkent. Oil-refining and the petro-chemical and pharmaceutical industries are developed. There are also cotton mills, astrakhan fur factories, and cement and brick works.

The province has 606 km. of railways and 5,000 km. of roads.

Taldy-Korgan

Area (sq. km.): 118,500
Population: 743,200
Persons per sq. km.: 6.3
Date of formation: 1944
Capital: Taldy-Korgan
No. of inhabitants: 127,000
Distance from Almaty: 258 km.

Located in the south-eastern part of the republic, the province was first formed in 1944, then abolished, then re-established in 1967. It borders on the Almaty, Semipalatinsk (Semey) and Jezkazgan provinces. Taldy-Korgan is divided into 12 administrative regions, and has five cities and 10 smaller urban settlements. The capital, which bears the same name, stands on the River Karatal.

The province lies south of lakes Balkhash and Alakol, with the Balkhash-Alakol depression occupying its central part. In the south of the province is the Ili valley, and in the north are ranges of sandy hills. In the eastern part, between the Jungar Alatau and the Barlyk range, is the mountain pass known as the Jungar Gate. The highest peak is Besbakan (4,442 m.). In the mountains there are 1,369 glaciers covering a total area of over 1,000 sq. km.

The most important natural resources are the large reserves of mixed metallic ores, marble and limestone. There are also deposits of hard and brown coal, oil shale, peat, gypsum, salt, tungsten and molybdenum.

The climate is continental, with moderately cold winters and hot, dry summers. On the shores of lakes Balkhash and Alakol, these are relieved by pleasant breezes.

The main rivers, fed by the glaciers, are the Ili, Karatal, Aksu and Lepsy, which all flow into Lake Balkhash. Alakol, and Jalanashkol are salt-water lakes, Sassykkol and Uyaly freshwater, while Balkash has both.

The sandy deserts, which are the main winter pastures, have large areas of saxaul thickets, grasses and scrub. On the shores of the lakes and in the water meadows by the rivers there are dense willow groves, poplar woods and thickets of tamarisk, reeds and rushes. Pastures with tall grass, woods of birch, apple trees and Tien-Shan fir are found on the mountain slopes and the plateaus. On the high alpine meadows, sedge, Altai violets and saxifrage grow. The wildlife includes hoofed animals, predators, various rodents and numerous species of birds. The rivers and lakes are abundant in fish.

The population consists of 360,500 Kazakhs (50.3%), 235,300 Russians (32.9%), 35,300 Germans (4.9%), 30,500 Uygurs (4.3%), 13,600 Koreans (1.9%), and smaller numbers of Ukrainians, Tatars, Belorussians, Azerbaijanis (Azeris), Kurds, Uzbeks and Dungans.

The main industrial sectors are non-ferrous metallurgy, the production of building materials, wood-working, the food industry and light industry. Power is based on transported coal.

The main branches of agriculture are irrigated farming, and livestock for meat and milk.

There are about 1,000 km. of railways in the province and 3,600 km. of roads.

Torgay

Area (sq. km.): 111,900
Population : 312,300
Persons per sq. km.: 2.7
Date of formation: 1988
Capital: Arkalyk
No. of inhabitants: 68,400
Distance from Almaty: 1,916 km.

This northern province was formed in 1970, abolished in 1988, then re-established in 1990. It is divided into 10 administrative regions, and has three cities and one smaller

287

urban settlement. The capital, Arkalyk, was founded in 1965.

A significant part of the territory lies on the Torgay plateau and the southern Torgay plain. In the north is the Ishim valley; in the south are the sandy massifs of Akkum and Tosynkum. The eastern part, on the western edge of the Sary Arka, with a succession of hills, plateaus and ravines, is the highest region of the province. The highest point is Kokshetau (478 m.).

There are deposits of coal, bauxite, iron ore, building materials and glass sand. The large reserves of bauxite provide the raw material for the Pavlodar aluminium works.

The climate is extreme continental. The deserts of Kazakhstan and Central Asia and also cold, dry, arctic air currents exert a strong influence on the climate. In winter, when there are strong winds and blizzards, the temperature can fall to 53°C below zero. In summer, which brings dry, hot winds, it can rise to 43°C. Precipitation is highest in summer.

There are 296 rivers, mostly small, on the territory of the province. The biggest are the Ishim and the Torgay. Their tributaries often cause flooding, but in summer they become shallow or dry up, turning into salt marshes. There is underground artesian water accumulated in the porous, sedimentary deposits.

The province is poor in flora. Meadows stretch along the shores of the lakes and in the lower regions of the south there are thickets of saxaul. The wildlife is that of the steppe and desert zones.

The sparse population consists of 127,000 Kazakhs (42.1%), 87,400 Russians (29%), 32,700 Ukrainians (10.8%), 14,400 Germans (4.82%), 9,500 Belorussians, 8,900 Tatars, and smaller numbers of Azerbaijanis, Bashkirs, Moldovians, Mari, Udmurts, Chuvash and Chechens. The main towns are Arkalyk, Esil and Derzhavinsk.

The province has a mixed agrarian and industrial economy. Industrial activity is mainly related to the extraction and processing of bauxite, and the mining of fire-resistant clays used in metallurgy. Agriculture is specialized in the production of grain, meat and wool.

There are 475 km. of railways and 4,000 km. of roads.

West Kazakhstan

Area (sq. km.): 151,200
Population: 659,900
Persons per sq. km.: 4.4
Date of formation: 1932
Capital: Uralsk
No. of inhabitants: 218,400
Distance from Almaty: 2,727 km.

This province in the north-western part of the republic, formed in 1932, was renamed the Ural province in 1962, but regained its former name of West Kazakhstan in 1992. It borders on the Orenburg, Kuibyshev, Saratov, Volgograd and Astrakhan provinces of the Russian Federation, and in the east on the Aktobe and Atyrau provinces of Kazakhstan. It is divided into 15 regions, and has three cities and four smaller urban settlements. The capital, Uralsk, on the River Ural, was probably founded in 1613, though some historical sources date its foundation, under the name of Yaik, to 1584. Since 1775 it has been called Uralsk.

A large part of its territory occupies the northern part of the Caspian lowlands with broad, sandy massifs and saline depressions. The southern part is intersected by dry valleys, forming an undulating plain. The highest point of the province is Aktau (263 m.).

Deposits of oil, gas, oil shale, various salts and building materials are found.

The climate is extreme continental: the mean temperature in January is 15°C, and in July, 26° C. The northern part is often swept by strong winds.

The main rivers are the Ural and its tributaries, which all freeze over in the middle of November. There are 144 freshwater and saline lakes. A series of reservoirs has been created to regulate the water supply in the southern part.

Vegetation is scanty on the bigger sandy massifs situated in the southern part. Poplar, oak, birch and willow grow in the water meadows along the rivers. There are wild goats, elks in the forests, wild boar in the reed thickets, and many species of birds. The rivers and lakes abound in fish.

The population is made up of 351,100 Kazakhs (55.8%), 216,500 Russians (34.4%), 28,100 Ukrainians (4.5%), 12,700 Tatars (2%), and smaller numbers of Belorussians, Germans, Mordvins and Chechens.

Grain growing and livestock raising are the most important branches of agriculture, in which the irrigation system, with a network of over 2,000 km., plays a major role. There are 15 million hectares of agricultural land, of which 2,124,900 hectares are arable land.

The energy sources are transported natural gas, coal and fuel oil. Over 90 industrial enterprises make a significant contribution to the province's economy.

West Kazakhstan has 417 km. of railways and 4,400 km. of roads.